James Buchanan

15th President of
the United States

Few men have entered the White House with higher expecta-
tions and a broader range of public service experience than
James Buchanan when he became the 15th President of the
United States on March 4, 1857. Yet four years later, there
was no chief executive happier to leave the office. (Library of
Congress.)

James Buchanan

15th President of the United States

David R. Collins

GARRETT EDUCATIONAL CORPORATION

Cover: *Official presidential portrait of James Buchanan by William M. Chase.* (Copyrighted by the White House Historical Association; photograph by the National Geographic Society.)

Manufactured in the United States of America

Edited and produced by Synthegraphics Corporation

Library of Congress Cataloging in Publication Data

Collins, David R.
 James Buchanan, 15th president of the United States / David R. Collins.
    p.   cm. — (Presidents of the United States)
 Includes bibliographical references.
 Summary: Presents the life of James Buchanan, including his childhood, education, employment, and political career.
 1. Buchanan, James, 1791–1868—Juvenile literature.
2. Presidents—United States—Biography—Juvenile literature. 3. United States—Politics and government—1857–1861—Juvenile literature.   [1. Buchanan, James, 1791–1868. 2. Presidents.]   I. Title.   II. Title: James Buchanan, fifteenth president of the United States. III. Series.
E437.C67   1990
973.6'8'092 — dc20
[B]
[92]   89-39948
ISBN 0-944483-62-3   CIP
                                                     AC

Contents

Chronology for
James Buchanan

1791 Born on April 23 in Cove Gap, Pennsylvania

1796 Moved to Mercersburg; attended public schools

1807– Attended Dickinson College in Carlisle,
1809 Pennsylvania

1812 Admitted to the bar; began law practice in Lancaster, Pennsylvania

1814 Served in a company of dragoons during War of 1812

1814– Served in Pennsylvania House of
1816 Representatives

1821– Served in U. S. House of Representatives
1831

1832– Served as U.S. minister to Russia
1833

1834– Served in U.S. Senate
1845

1845– Served as secretary of state under
1849 President James Knox Polk

1849 Retired to Wheatland, his estate near Lancaster, Pennsylvania

1853 Served as minister to Great Britain

1857– Served as President of the United States
1861

1868 Died on June 1 at Wheatland

Chapter 1

A Major Miscalculation

Pulling his muffler slightly higher around his neck, a lone figure hurried across the floor of a hotel lobby in Washington, D.C. It was clear that the man did not wish to be noticed, certainly not recognized by the small group of seven patrons nearby. But there was little danger of that. Comfortably nestled in overstuffed chairs, the group of four men and three women were engaged in a heated discussion.

The topic they were discussing was a familiar one – in the nation's capital and far beyond – for the year was 1857, and in any gathering one was most likely to hear talk about slavery. In this case, the specific topic being discussed was the book *Uncle Tom's Cabin;* its author, Harriet Beecher Stowe; and just how much the volume had contributed to the controversy over slavery.

In the shadows, James Buchanan listened for a few minutes, then went to his room. He carried his own secret about slavery from Rogert B. Taney, the Chief Justice of the U.S. Supreme Court, but Buchanan would not share it with anyone until after his presidential inauguration.

A FATAL ACCIDENT

Several blocks away, a weary Franklin Pierce sat quietly reading papers on his White House desk. In another week he would turn over the duties of the presidency to another, and Pierce was grateful. The strong foreign policy he had hoped to achieve had never materialized, while sectional splits on the domestic scene threatened to rip the country apart. The handsome and amiable man from New Hampshire had failed in many of his hopes and those of his Democratic Party. Perhaps, if there had not been the accident . . . .

A "dark horse" (an unexpected candidate) at the Democratic National Convention in 1852, Pierce had managed to beat out the party favorites—Lewis Cass, Stephen A. Douglas, and James Buchanan—for the presidential nomination. Then, in the November election, Pierce won the presidency by defeating General Winfield Scott, who could not pull together the badly split Whig Party. Following the election, Franklin Pierce eagerly awaited the moment when he would assume leadership as the nation's chief executive.

But two months after the national election and two months before the inauguration, tragedy struck. As Franklin and Jane Pierce were returning to their New Hampshire home from Boston with their son Benjamin, the railroad car in which they were riding overturned. Although neither parent was injured, 11-year-old Benjamin was killed.

Having already lost two older sons at early ages, the death of their only living child was devastating. Mrs. Pierce wore black the entire four years of her husband's administration, and she refused to attend any official events. Deeply religious, the couple lived in quiet seclusion during their White House years, with Franklin never regaining the enthusiasm for his duties that he had displayed before the accident.

A New Leader

It was, therefore, perhaps no great surprise that the Washington community prepared to welcome the country's new leader with much cheerful ceremony. Already under construction was a special building on Judiciary Square which would cost a hearty $15,000 when finished. An inaugural supper would be served in one of the building's two rooms, while the second would be totally devoted to serving as a giant ballroom. Red, white, and blue walls the building would have, with golden stars studded on a white ceiling. There were rumors of invitations being sold, with the added admonition that "the old man better not get wind of it."

The "old man" was James Buchanan, of course, who would become the 15th President of the United States on March 4, 1857. At age 65, he brought to the executive branch over 40 years of public service as a congressman, senator, Cabinet member, and foreign diplomat. Methodical and efficient, he was not known for any particular polish as an orator or flamboyancy in style. Instead, he had risen to the country's highest office through diligent "plodding"—accepting a responsibility and carrying it out to the best of his ability.

An impeccable dresser, Buchanan always sat and stood with courtly bearing, his six-foot frame well distributed. An eye defect caused him to tilt his head forward and sideways when conversing. This would make most people think he was extremely interested in what they were saying, and they felt deeply complimented.

The President's Niece

Buchanan's election as President in the fall of 1856 caused many in Washington society to wonder if the White House might continue to maintain the same somber tone it had for

Harriet Lane served as official White House hostess for her bachelor uncle, President James Buchanan. Congenial and bright, she carried out similar duties when he was the American ambassador to Great Britain. On both sides of the Atlantic, she proved a favorite among the people and the press. (Library of Congress.)

the past four years. Not that James Buchanan was any kind of wallflower. Indeed, he was said to add sparkling conversation to any dinner party or dance. But as a bachelor, he brought no First Lady to the White House, so most assumed that entertaining in the executive manor would be held to a minimum. That notion was soon put to rest, however, as word circulated around the capital city that the President's niece, Miss Harriet Lane, would be serving as the official White House hostess.

Daughter of James Buchanan's sister Jane, Harriet was only seven years old when her mother died, then two years later she lost her father. "Uncle James" had done much to raise the child and now, in her mid-twenties, Harriet volunteered to carry out whatever social duties were asked of her. She was known to enjoy a spirited dinner gathering and was not opposed to dancing. Happily, it appeared that the somber years of the Pierce administration would soon be disappearing.

A One-Term President

But as for James Buchanan himself, his mind was far removed from dinner parties and dances. As his niece and aides busied themselves with the planning for the gala inaugural, the President-elect contemplated more serious matters. He had already decided that he would put himself above party squabbling by announcing that he would be a one-term President. Under no circumstances would he put himself in the same position as Pierce, allowing the Democrats to turn away from him at convention time and select another candidate. No, Buchanan was proud — some claimed arrogant — and he would never permit himself to face that kind of public humiliation.

The federal coffers were filled to overflowing; the United States Treasury never before had enjoyed such an enviable financial status. At least, Buchanan knew, he would not have to worry about rebuilding the country's economy.

Fresh from service as the United States minister (ambassador) to Great Britain, Buchanan had found special adventure and excitement in dealing with international affairs. With his American ministerial colleagues in France and Spain, Buchanan had tried hard to persuade Spain to sell Cuba to the United States. This attempt had whetted Buchanan's appetite for acquiring new lands for the United States. He relished the thought that, as President, he might be able not only to purchase Cuba, but Alaska as well. Russia did not enjoy the same financial security that the United States was experiencing, and Buchanan felt that if the price was right, the United States could buy Alaska from Russia.

The Slavery Issue

Before his inauguration, James Buchanan worked day after day at his estate near Lancaster, Pennsylvania. "Wheatland," as his home was called, always afforded him the comfort and peace he needed for careful contemplation. But it did not provide Buchanan with the direct and secretive channels he needed for meeting the most important challenge facing his presidency. No matter how much the United States Treasury overflowed, no matter how many new lands could be acquired by the United States, if the slavery issue was not resolved and the union of states preserved, the administration of James Buchanan would be a blemish in the annals of American history.

No one was more conscious of this fact than Buchanan himself, who had no intention of having his name associated with failure. Whatever needed to be done to guarantee the stability of the country and the success of his term in office—within the framework of the Constitution, of course—

Buchanan was willing to do. With this in mind, he left Wheatland for Washington, D.C., late in February of 1857.

THE DRED SCOTT CASE

Despite the accepted separation of the executive and judicial branches of government, James Buchanan was determined to find out the outcome of one case presently being decided by the Supreme Court. Although such action was not illegal, it certainly was unethical. But in taking over the leadership of the nation, Buchanan felt he had to do whatever was necessary in order to be properly prepared. It was this awareness that made the President-elect seek information about the case from Chief Justice Roger Taney. Buchanan was convinced that the solidarity of the United States could depend upon the outcome of the case, which involved a slave named Dred Scott.

The Dred Scott case actually started in 1834. An Army surgeon, Dr. John Emerson, moved his family and servants from St. Louis, Missouri, to Rock Island, Illinois, where he worked at the national arsenal there. Included in the Emerson household was a slave named Dred Scott. Due to a 1787 congressional ruling outlawing slavery in Illinois, keeping Scott as a slave was illegal. But there was no mention of this while Emerson and Scott remained in Illinois.

A few years later, Emerson moved again, being transferred to Fort Snelling in the Wisconsin Territory. Although the Missouri Compromise of 1820 had outlawed slavery in the territory, nothing was said to Scott, who continued to work as a slave.

Suing for Freedom

Shortly after returning to St. Louis in 1846, Dr. Emerson died. His widow subsequently remarried, and the ownership of Dred Scott, under Missouri law, passed to the widow's brother,

John Sanford of New York. A St. Louis attorney, aware of the situation, persuaded Dred Scott to sue for his freedom, claiming he had lived for several years in free territory.

Slowly the case ground its way through the lower courts, some judges supporting the rights of Dred Scott and others claiming he had no rights at all. Finally, the case reached the Supreme Court. It was no secret that the ultimate decision would have great bearing on the state of the Union. Certainly James Buchanan recognized its importance, and as he stood to deliver his inaugural address, he had a secret. He already knew the results of the Dred Scott case, and without revealing specific information, he called upon all Americans to readily accept the decisions of the highest court in the land.

Two days later, the Supreme Court announced its decision. Although it was a seven to two decision, with each of the nine judges offering a separate opinion, the majority of thought fell in line with Chief Justice Taney. The ruling supported two basic principles. (1) Being a slave, Dred Scott was not an American citizen. Therefore, he could not legally bring any suit into federal courts. (2) Although he had lived in federal territory closed to slavery, the Missouri Compromise prohibition was unconstitutional. Under the Fifth Amendment, slaves were considered property. Therefore, Congress could not pass any law that would take property away from citizens, so concluded the judges of the Court.

An Angry Reaction

"Taney hates slavery as I do," Buchanan confided to an aide. "But this is a matter beyond the personal feelings of the President and the Chief Justice of the United States. The matter is settled. The Constitution shall be upheld, and we can move on to other concerns."

Buchanan's hopes were soon cast to the wind. Southern

leaders immediately spoke out in support of the Supreme Court decision, declaring it "wise and fair." But slavery opponents in the North, mostly Republicans, denounced the Court's opinion and promised to gain control of the government, change the composition of the Court, and have the Dred Scott decision overturned.

As for Buchanan himself, he was shocked at the reaction. Always the calm political practitioner, he was the most outstanding constitutional lawyer of the times. He knew that the Dred Scott decision would not please everyone, but he had miscalculated just how angry some Americans would be. As he put together his Cabinet, he deliberately selected three northerners, three southerners, and one from Tennessee, an in-between state. But there was little he could do to quell the outrage that lingered. Members of Congress were furious that the Supreme Court should engage in any political controversy, particularly by stating that the Missouri Compromise was unconstitutional.

"We are elected representatives of the people," one congressman challenged. "If we cannot outlaw slavery in a territory, neither can a territorial legislature. The idea of popular sovereignty, people determining whether they have slavery or not, no longer exists."

"Sitting on a Volcano"

The Supreme Court stood firm, aghast that their decision would be so openly challenged, and with such hostility. "If we are to be a nation of law and honor," Chief Justice Taney retorted, "the final decisions of the Supreme Court must be upheld, whether they please a majority or a minority."

Deeply disappointed, James Buchanan felt the burden of the presidency from the very beginning of his term. Always the brightest, smiling face around the White House, his niece Harriet could seldom bring a smile to the face of the man she truly idolized and wished to make happy. "One cannot dwell on things we cannot change," the young woman philosophized. "One should try to find joy in the beauty of life."

They were cheerful thoughts, but James Buchanan found them fleeting. It was the words of Edwin Stanton of Ohio that rang ever more true as to the situation surrounding the chief executive. "You are sitting on a volcano," Stanton told Buchanan one morning at a breakfast meeting.

Wearily, the President nodded. He felt old and tired, sometimes wondering wistfully why he had ever left his quiet and secure Wheatland home. How peaceful were those days in Pennsylvania, especially those times so long ago when the only noise that intruded on a warm summer day was the tinkling doorbell of his father's shop in Mercersburg.

Chapter 2

"A Clever and Spirited Youth"

T he year 1791 seemed a most suitable time for James Buchanan to make his appearance in the world. George Washington was in his first term as President, four million people were divided among 14 states, and the Supreme Court met for the first time. Nine out of 10 families farmed; the few which did not relied on producing home-made crafts and serving the public to make a living. James Buchanan, Sr., an immigrant from County Donegal, Ireland, fell into the latter category. He had come to America shortly before the peace treaty with England was signed in 1783.

After staying for a time with relatives in Philadelphia, James Buchanan, Sr., then looked for a good business loca-tion. He came upon a trading area called Cove Gap, about 40 miles west of Philadelphia. A bustling stopover for set-tlers heading to Pittsburgh, Buchanan began bringing in goods from Baltimore and selling them. His business prospered.

THE BUCHANANS OF COVE GAP

By the spring of 1788, James Buchanan, Sr., felt financially secure enough to marry Elizabeth Speer, a farm girl six years his junior. Ten months later, they welcomed their first child,

James Buchanan, Jr., was born in this log cabin on April 23, 1791. He lived here until 1796. Restored and strengthened against weathering, the Buchanan cabin is presently located on the campus of Mercersburg Academy in Pennsylvania. (Library of Congress.)

a daughter named Mary. A son was born on April 23, 1791, and promptly named James, Jr., after his father. By the end of that same year, however, death had taken Mary, and the two parents showered their attention totally on James, Jr. Although James, Sr., and Elizabeth would eventually have nine more children, they would have no more sons for another 14 years.

A Prospering Business

Both Mr. Buchanan and his wife Elizabeth took their Scotch-Irish ancestry and their Presbyterian faith seriously in the raising of their children. Young James Buchanan grew up in a home where love was attached to responsibility and duty.

The trading post at Cove Gap expanded and prospered. Soon the elder Buchanan not only ran a store but also owned the surrounding log cabins, stables, farm lands, an orchard, and a storehouse. The prosperity brought problems, however, as the increased traffic posed dangers for the expanding Buchanan family. In 1796, with two children and another on the way, Mr. Buchanan bought a 300-acre parcel of land near Mercersburg, some five miles away. In the center of town, he purchased a two-story brick structure that could serve as a home and a store.

EARLY EDUCATION

As soon as he was tall enough to see over the counter, young James was clerking in his father's store. Customers were amused by the boy; they were also amazed at how quickly he could add figures and how well he could converse with adults. Praise for his son was nimbly handled by Mr. Buchanan, who had little desire to encourage any trace of vanity in the boy.

Living in Mercersburg also offered young James the opportunity for formal schooling. Not that he had gone uneducated in his earliest years, for Elizabeth was unique for her times. Although she had never been to school, she loved to read. John Milton, Samuel Johnson, Alexander Pope—all great British writers—were shared with her children, along with a heavy diet of Scripture readings and Bible study.

James received the lion's share of such learning, being the only boy. Girls of the day were only expected to read and write enough that they might communicate through social letters. Boys, however, were expected to use their reading and writing skills to seek a profession. While young Buchanan spent his extra moments perfecting his script on a slate, the girls in the family learned to cook, knit, can, and sew.

As soon as James was old enough, he was enrolled in the grammar school in Mercersburg. His home schooling held him in good stead, and he moved rapidly into more advanced lessons of study. "His mind is quick, his behavior courteous," an appreciative James Sharon, the schoolmaster, told James' parents. Similar reports came from Dr. Jesse Magaw, who led the eager scholar into classical literature and ancient history.

Methodical, Meticulous, and Self-Disciplined

Methodical and meticulous, James not only learned well from instructors, but he acquired self-discipline. In a diary, he kept daily records of everything he did. At his father's store, he carefully supervised the accounting of every penny brought in. Despite his attention to store business, he nonetheless enjoyed the lively discussions that took place among customers. Advocates of both major political parties, the Democratic-Republicans and the Federalists, ranted and raved about the events of the day. For the most part, James sided with his father, supporting President Washington and the Federalists.

Occasionally, a traveler would leave behind a newspaper. Young Buchanan would then stay up all night reading the periodical word for word. He prided himself on being able to quote stories exactly in the days that followed.

English, Latin, Greek—James displayed special strengths in these major academic areas. He passed swiftly from one educational plateau to another. His excellence at the Old Stone Academy grammar school constantly placed him at the head of his class, and in 1807, he was admitted to Dickinson College in Carlisle, Pennsylvania, as a junior. He was only 16 years old.

COLLEGE YEARS

Once at Dickinson, James wasted no time in showing that he was a leader in classroom activities. And he was a creative mischief-maker, too. His classmates seemed to have little use for hard study, preferring to find more cheerful ways to occupy their time. Buchanan notes in his diary that he joined them "in order to be considered a clever and spirited youth."

James often led small bands of his comrades on midnight excursions across the small Dickinson campus. Drinking and smoking lifted his courage. All too often the reckless young Buchanan found himself the subject of disciplinary actions. He was a constant source of irritation to his instructors, who knew of his bad behavior and yet noted that he scored the highest marks in his classes.

Expelled!

After completing his junior year at Dickinson, James returned home to help his father. As they sat one September morning studying the store accounts, a letter arrived from the college.

While the senior Buchanan opened the envelope and read its contents, James tried to concentrate on the numbers in front of him. Wearing a pained expression, the elder Buchanan put the letter down and left the room.

Quickly James picked up the letter and read it; he felt sick to his stomach. Due to his "improprieties," he was not going to be able to return to Dickinson. It was only out of respect for his father that the school had allowed his son to finish the first year at the college.

Dickinson College meant little to young James Buchanan. But the awareness that he had tainted the family name by his behavior caused him to feel great personal shame. Immediately he went to their family pastor, Dr. John King, and sought his advice. Not only was Dr. King a respected theologian throughout Pennsylvania, he was also a trustee at Dickinson College.

"If I intercede in your behalf," Dr. King told James, "you must promise me that you will behave properly during your senior year. There can be no more 'improprieties' of any kind." Gratefully, the contrite student agreed.

Graduation

Young James Buchanan kept his word. Whenever the urge for merrymaking came along, he remembered the pledge he had made to Dr. King and the respect he owed to his father. He studied constantly, led class discussions, and sailed through the oral examinations administered by the professors at the end of the school term. Clearly, he was eligible to receive scholastic honors at the graduation exercises.

But that was not to be. In spite of his academic achievements, James Buchanan, Jr., had been too much of a troublemaker. To honor him at graduation would be an insult to his professors and the school – at least, so the college leaders felt. Disappointed, James decided that he would not attend commencement. But when several faculty members personally contacted him, urging him to attend, he agreed.

In 1809 James graduated from Dickinson, but he would never have any good feelings about the school. His father was equally disappointed, stating, "The more you know of mankind, the more you will distrust them. It is said that the knowledge of mankind and the distrust of them are reciprocally connected."

CHOOSING A CAREER

At 18 years of age, James was ready to choose a career. If his mother would have had her way, he would likely have gone into the ministry. "There is no greater service, no grander calling than that of the Lord," she said often. But as devout a Presbyterian as Mr. Buchanan was, he did not encourage his son toward becoming a minister.

Each passing day brought news of building and land sales. People were moving west and needed sound legal advice for selling what they owned. More and more lawyers were needed to handle the paperwork required, and the senior Buchanan was convinced his son would make a fine attorney.

James saw no need to rush his decision. Anyway, he wanted to put aside the unhappy memories of his final days at Dickinson. For months he roamed the woods around Mercersburg, hunting squirrels and rabbits for the family stewpot. He chopped wood and helped repair his father's buildings.

His six-foot frame boasted new strength and muscle; his skin, a healthy handsome glow.

Becoming a Lawyer

By December, James had made up his mind. He would follow the path his father had selected and become a lawyer. Arrangements were made to clerk with James Hopkins, an attorney in Lancaster, a bustling city of 6,000 people. James packed a trunk, boarded a stagecoach, and headed for Lancaster, the capital of Pennsylvania at that time.

Once in Lancaster, young Buchanan took lodging in Widow Duchman's Inn. The clean and attractive location strained the law clerk's meager earnings. But being near the city square and in the shadow of the courthouse, Buchanan was in the middle of the town's activity, caught up in the swirl of daily events. "Each day I see people of prominence," he wrote home to his family. "Unfortunately, I see them on the street and not in our law offices."

Avoiding "Wasteful Amusements"

The hours were long and grueling in Hopkins' service, yet Buchanan put in extra hours reading and rereading law books. At times he was lured by the taverns in Lancaster, a temptation he shared openly with his father through correspondence. The older Buchanan wrote back firm warnings against such "wasteful amusements," and encouraged his son to "dedicate total heart and spirit to the profession you have chosen." It was clear Mr. Buchanan wanted no repetition of the Dickinson College days.

James took his father's advice seriously, devoting himself to the study of law whether he was at the office or not. When he was not involved in legal cases or pouring over law books, he went for long walks in the woods of Lancaster. With only the forest creatures listening, the young law clerk practiced reciting the laws and arguments he had heard and studied all day. Not only did it make him more familiar with complicated legal statutes, such nightly strolls provided time to master skills of public speaking. At times, Buchanan would imagine himself presenting a case before the Supreme Court.

Passing the Bar

After spending three years in his law office, Hopkins told James it was time to seek admission to the bar. He did so and became a practicing attorney in November of 1812. However, few people in Lancaster noticed the small announcement in the newspaper, as most were caught up in the latest news of the war against England, which had begun a few months before.

Early in 1813, the new lawyer opened up his own offices near the Widow Duchman's Inn. He also won an appointment as a deputy prosecutor for Lancaster County. Although most thought Buchanan to be an able attorney, little business came his way. When a Federalist friend approached him about running for state representative early in 1814, Buchanan willingly consented. He was certainly not becoming rich practicing law; perhaps politics might open new doors. But first there was a war to be fought.

Joining the Dragoons

Buchanan, like most Federalists, had little interest at first in the war effort. Most bemoaned the fact that "Madison, that midget in the White House, was a far cry from the Washington, Adams and yes, although he was a Democratic-Republican, Jefferson, that preceded him." But when word swept westward that the British had burned the nation's capital and were marching toward Baltimore, loyalty to political parties dissolved.

A meeting was called in Lancaster Square to rally volunteers for a trip to "drive the British home!" One after another, men leaped to the podium to vent their patriotic passion aloud, then sign a list of those who would serve. "We are not Federalists or Democratic-Republicans in this encounter," Buchanan shouted, his voice well tuned in oratorical declamation. "We are Americans, united in our efforts to send those trespassers away from our shores. Let us become a wall of unconquerable power and spirit."

Quickly the enlistment scroll was covered with names. The volunteers elected a captain from among their own ranks and decided to be dragoons, soldiers on horseback who would carry short muskets. With such arms, they could serve either as a cavalry or as an infantry fighting force.

Eager to join the battle, the Lancaster County Dragoons organized quickly and headed east to Baltimore. As they rode, their hearty voices filled the air with spirited yelps and cheers. But if they had hoped to see active service or any military encounter, they were to be disappointed. Because Major Charles Ridgely needed horses more than he needed soldiers, Buchanan and his men were assigned to bring in "any rideable mare or stallion, obtained in any way possible." It was not the dramatic mission the dragoons had hoped for, but they were satisfied that their contribution was necessary. Once the British were out of Baltimore, the men from Lancaster headed back home to their regular lives.

ENTERING POLITICS

Caught up in the fervor of patriotic spirit, Buchanan had almost forgotten about the thought of running for state representative—almost, but not quite. His willingness to defend his country as a dragoon put him in good stead with the voters, despite the meager contributions of the men from Lancaster County. He ran on the Federalist ticket, scoring an easy victory.

Always a stern skeptic, James Buchanan, Sr., questioned whether it was a prudent decision for James, Jr., to leave a beginning law practice and enter the political arena. But for the younger Buchanan, there was little doubt that he was doing the right thing. He had always enjoyed the political discussions that took place in his father's store in Mercersburg. And his happiest moments at Dickenson College had been during class debates and discussions. As a lawyer, he discovered himself analyzing every issue and every case from different points of view. And, brief as the excursion was with the Lancaster County Dragoons, he was thoroughly caught up with the thought of fighting for ideas. Yes, indeed, James Buchanan Jr. was ready to enter the world of politics.

Chapter 3

Inside the Statehouse

James arrived in the new Pennsylvania capital city of Harrisburg with mixed emotions. The War of 1812 still continued with the British, now rumored to be planning an attack on Philadelphia. Buchanan was delighted he was in the midst of the action. At the same time, being a newly elected representative to the legislature, he had little knowledge of how the state government operated and what part he could play in it. The representative from Lancaster promised to be an attentive listener and an observer before sharing his thoughts on an issue.

Day after day, Buchanan attended legislative sessions, soaking in the sounds and sights around him. He noted those eloquent speakers who shared their ideas with clarity and purpose, and he carefully studied the reactions of those who listened. He learned, too, from those representatives who rambled aimlessly and lost themselves and their audience through their own disjointed messages. Often he took notes on both the good and the bad of what he observed, and he pledged to imitate only the strong, convincing speakers when the time came for him to make a speech.

ADDRESSING HIS COLLEAGUES

That opportunity came in 1815, as the rumor of a British attack on Philadelphia approached certainty. How could the port city be protected? Representatives offered different plans for conscription (military service). One major program called for all men in the state to be divided into groups of 22, between the ages of 18 and 45. One man in the group would be chosen to serve in the Army, while the remaining 21 would raise $200 for his salary or bounty. After a year's service, a new name would be drawn and another bounty raised. The Army would be paid by the state. Another major plan called for three years of service by six regiments of volunteers. No money would be required from those not in service.

By the time he rose to speak, young Buchanan was well prepared. Before taking a stand on either of the two plans suggested, he lashed out at the federal government for engaging in a war without seeking the support of state treasuries. As to the programs of conscription, he endorsed the plan for volunteers, calling the other suggestion totally unfair. He argued that the eastern part of the state, in which Philadelphia was located, was rich and well settled. "The raising of $200 among such residents would pose no hardship at all," Buchanan observed. "But the western section is still frontier, inhabited primarily by poor farmers. Two hundred dollars would be a fortune, probably impossible to raise among twenty-one men or twenty-one hundred." Buchanan pleaded for a more democratic means of putting together an army, a call for volunteers.

Completing his remarks, Buchanan sat down. He was satisfied with his first talk before his fellow representatives, and the scattered applause testified that there were others who supported his remarks. Yet there was much more debate to follow, in both the Pennsylvania House of Representatives and the Senate. By the time the issue came up for a vote, the

This picture of Buchanan was painted in 1847, while he was serving as secretary of state. When in his early twenties, Buchanan got his first taste of politics by serving in the Pennsylvania House of Representatives. He was determined not to let either an eye defect or a lifelong liver ailment hinder his career. (Library of Congress.)

representatives, much to Buchanan's delight, passed the bill calling for volunteers. The senators, however, passed the financial conscription plan. Thankfully, before the entire matter was raised again, the war ended and the matter died out.

Although the issue was soon forgotten, James Buchanan's speech was not. To one of the Democratic-Republicans (later to become the Democratic Party), the vibrant young representative from Lancaster had sounded like one of their own party members. "Why call yourself a Federalist when you clearly are one of us?" the political leader asked. "Come join us."

Buchanan was stunned. Why, he had never thought of himself as anything but a Federalist. It was obvious his ideas were misunderstood. "I would not even consider such a thought!" Buchanan declared. Nonetheless, the encounter was not soon forgotten. Returning to Lancaster after his first term, Buchanan wondered if his own constituents also had questions as to his political position. He had been elected as a Federalist; would he still have strength on that ticket?

An Easy Win

Surprisingly, Buchanan's decision as to whether or not to run again for state representative was influenced by his father's encouragement to do so. James, Jr., made no secret of the fact that he could earn over $2,000 in 1815 from his law practice, more than he had ever earned in his life. Politics had expanded his personal contacts and business opportunities. "If a man's work is a source of comfortable income and offers contentment as well, why would one wish to change?" his father wrote. The elder Buchanan did, however, suggest that his son might want to consider running for the U.S. Congress, if he wished to continue in public life.

After James decided to run for re-election to the state

legislature, he eagerly accepted an invitation to address the Washington Association of Lancaster on Independence Day, 1815. It would provide him with the opportunity to clear up any misconceptions that the public may have had about his political allegiances. Almost before the band stopped playing and he was introduced, Buchanan was on his feet, attacking President James Madison and the U.S. Congress for their inept actions during the War of 1812. Never had he put more into a presentation, his blond hair framing his fiery red face. "Never again should we allow such a bloody stain to mar the pages of America's history books!" the spirited orator exclaimed.

Buchanan drew lengthy cheering and applause from those who sat beneath the speaker's platform that day, but it was not until later that he learned his explosive remarks had damaged his image as well. Some felt that an Independence Day ceremony was an inappropriate occasion for such a partisan speech, while Democratic-Republicans and even some Federalists felt that his comments were too harsh. "Perhaps," Buchanan noted in his journal, "a tone of moderation would have been more effective."

Whatever the case, Buchanan was an easy winner in the October 1815 elections and returned to Harrisburg. The major issue facing the state legislature was no longer military defense; it was the dilemma of banking and effective control of currency.

RECHARTERING THE NATIONAL BANK

Money had always been a problem in the United States since its founding. Paper money was issued by the Continental Congress during the Revolutionary War period, but few people placed much worth in it because there were no national funds to back it up. Then, before the government had a chance to become financially sound in the late 1700s and early 1800s, the War of 1812 came along and required the building of an expensive Navy to fight against the British. Again, paper money was issued by the federal government from banks scattered among the states.

Because each of the states also wrote its own laws concerning the issuing of money, people were again skeptical of the true value of circulating paper money. Most individuals preferred to be paid in coins or to barter for goods. Business and government leaders from other countries were even more distrustful, refusing to accept any payment for imports unless it was in gold or silver. "Paste your paper money on your walls," sneered one foreign merchant. "It is more decorative than it is anything else."

The first National Bank of the United States had been chartered by Congress in 1791 and was to run for 20 years. Due to the dramatic events preceding the War of 1812, the charter had not been renewed. With the war over, rechartering the national bank became an issue at the federal level, and even trickled down to the various state legislatures.

President James Madison came out forcefully against rechartering the national bank system. "It puts too much power in the hands of too few," he argued. However, such political leaders as Congressman John C. Calhoun of South Carolina and Henry Clay of Kentucky retorted, "Without a national bank, we shall never restore a sound currency system to the country." Buchanan studied the arguments, analyzing each point with much care, and favored Madison's position. He was aware that the Federalists largely endorsed the rechartering of the bank, and it troubled him that he was again somewhat out of step with his political party. Perhaps he should investigate further, to see if he were better suited to the Democratic-Republicans. He promised himself to do so.

In the meantime, however, Buchanan's second term in the state legislature proved to be less fulfilling than the first. The banking issue was tiring and tedious, and when Congress voted for rechartering the national bank in 1816, whatever controversy and drama it had evaporated. Buchanan returned to Lancaster at the end of his second term, no longer interested in further service as a state representative. He was grateful that his father agreed with the decision.

BUILDING A REPUTATION

Both as an attorney and as a state legislator, James Buchanan had built a reputation of honesty, preparedness, and general knowledge of all areas of law. He attracted many clients, who were immediately impressed by his confident bearing and fashionable clothes. "It is imperative that a lawyer display the best of manners and the most handsome appearance possible," Buchanan once told an associate. "Both a client and a judge notice such things."

If there was any criticism of Buchanan in his handling of civil and criminal cases, it could be that he provided too many details, too much documentation. One judge summoned the attorney to his chambers and admonished Buchanan for taking too long in making his points. "You had the case won in the first hour," the wordy lawyer was told, "and yet you took the entire day for your presentation. Sometimes less is better than more."

Defending a Judge

A great deal of publicity came to Buchanan late in 1818, when efforts were made to impeach a Pennsylvania judge. The case involved a militiaman who had been called into service by the federal government. When the judge ruled that the state had no power in such a matter, there was a loud outcry of states' rights advocates.

In addition to the argument of whose power was greater, the state's or the federal government's, Buchanan also sensed devious political maneuvering among Pennsylvania Democratic-Republicans to remove a Federalist judge from office. Enjoying the challenge, Buchanan took the case and skillfully defended his client. As a result, he gained more newspaper coverage in this one trial than he had while serving two terms in the state legislature.

Buchanan's victory brought a herd of public officials, all facing impeachment for one reason or another, hurrying to his law office. By the summer of 1819, Buchanan had accumulated a modest fortune for the times while regularly sending money home to his father. More than one unmarried woman in the Lancaster community gazed wistfully at the 28-year-old, blond, six-foot attorney, who was said to have "a brilliant legal mind and a social wit besides." As for Buchanan, he was giving more and more thought to finding someone with whom he could share his success and who would become his wife.

A TRAGIC ROMANCE

Ann Coleman was the daughter of a wealthy iron-mill owner in Lancaster. After meeting each other at the home of a mutual friend, Buchanan and the cheerful Miss Coleman spent many evenings together. No longer did the Lancaster attorney frequent the dingy inns and boisterous taverns of earlier years. Together, the couple enjoyed a more elegant life-style, such as romantic candlelight suppers and attending poetry readings. Wintertime brought sleigh rides and group sings with other young people of the city.

Ann was clearly more captivated by her suitor than was her father. Robert Coleman was afraid that Buchanan might be just as interested in the family wealth as he was in his daughter. The young woman dismissed such notions, but she was troubled over Buchanan's intense interest in his profession. Nonetheless, in the summer of 1819, the couple became engaged.

As plans for the wedding progressed, stories reached Ann that Buchanan had been seen in the company of another woman. Confronted with the accusation, Buchanan admitted it, but claimed it was neither a loving nor a lasting relationship. Thinking that her father's suspicions might be justified, Ann broke the engagement. It was a painful blow to Buchanan, who suffered even further when Ann refused to see him again or answer his letters. He continued to write throughout the autumn of 1819, hoping that she might reconsider.

In December, Buchanan learned that Ann had gone to visit her sister in Philadelphia. Soon after, word was received that she had died from an overdose of medicine. Rumors circulated that Ann had committed suicide, a thought that greatly troubled Buchanan. He wrote to her family, begging to join the mourners at the funeral, but his letter was returned unanswered.

RETURN TO POLITICS

Anguished, James left Lancaster by stagecoach, retreating to the comfort and support of his family in Mercersburg. He wrote, "I feel that happiness has fled from me forever," and went for long walks through the woods that he had known as a child. He dreaded the return to Lancaster, but knew that eventually he would have to go back. Haunted by memories of happier days, he seriously considered leaving the area.

A more specific opportunity arose in the spring of 1820, when James was approached by representatives of the Federalist Party. "We need a candidate to run for the United States Congress," the visitors explained, "representing Lancaster, York and Dauphin Counties. Would you be willing?" Ordinarily, Buchanan would have refused. Recollections of his service in the state legislature were not that favorable. Yet, should he run and win, it would be a way of getting out of Lancaster. Grateful for the chance, Buchanan accepted.

As was his custom, James carefully studied each and every issue before making his first campaign speech. He was delighted to discover that people remembered his effective service in the state legislature. When the election was held in the fall of 1820, the young attorney from Lancaster scored a lopsided victory. Since the next session of Congress was not scheduled to convene until December of 1821, Buchanan had plenty of time to close out pressing legal matters with his clients in Lancaster.

As a surprise, James hoped to convince his father to accompany him to Washington when he was sworn into office as a U.S. congressman. But tragedy intervened. On June 11, 1821, James Buchanan, Sr., was killed in a carriage accident. With four children still at home, Elizabeth Speer Buchanan faced a dismal future, a situation greatly eased by her eldest son's promise to "help in every way possible."

Chapter 4
Learning the Game

W hen Buchanan arrived in Washington in November 1821, his mind bulged with statistics. From the moment he had been declared the winner of the election held the year before, he had been cramming himself full of information he considered necessary to represent his Pennsylvania constituents effectively.

Serving in the state legislature was one thing. James would gather opinions and thoughts from those with whom he had daily contact in Lancaster. He then carried the ideas into the governmental chambers in Harrisburg. But the role of a national congressman in Washington demanded an awareness of matters and events much greater in geographical range and historical concept. There might be other congressmen who could boast better educations and more diverse experiences, but James Buchanan personally pledged himself to be ready and able to attend to any legislative issue brought before him.

AN ERA OF GOOD FEELING

The seriousness of Buchanan's mood contrasted somewhat with the general mood of the country. This particular period in American history has been called "The Era of Good Feeling," due largely to a positive atmosphere generated by President James Monroe in the White House. Trade with other countries was booming, the national economy was mushrooming, and American pioneers were traveling west with a spirit of hope and enthusiasm. Both the population and the number of states were growing, the former to almost 10,000,000 and the latter to 23.

Immigrants poured into the country, most settling in northern cities, where they worked as cheap laborers. Although eight out of ten Americans still made their living from farming at the time Buchanan reached Congress, urban areas were growing in size and number. But there were still pioneer families that trudged westward in search of open spaces and cheap land.

As Buchanan traveled to Washington, he met many people headed west. "Each face I saw seemed to radiate a glow of expectation," the congressman-elect noted, "as if the next valley would beckon each one of these folks into a glorious homeland. In truth, I knew they were headed into wilderness, but never would I have stolen their dreams."

The Missouri Compromise

Having read almost every available periodical before going to the nation's capital, Buchanan knew in advance what problems lay ahead. The issue of slavery, not just the practice itself but rather as an acceptable condition under which new states were being admitted to the Union, was of paramount concern. In 1820, Missouri posed just such a problem— whether it should be admitted as a free state or as a slave state. After much heated argument, Congress settled the question, at least for the time being.

Slavery in America

There are those who speak with loud and proud voices of a nation welcoming immigrants from countries around the world, and yet those same voices lose volume when discussing the millions of African slaves brought into the United States. Beginning with some ''20 and odd negars'' that arrived in Jamestown, Virginia, in 1619, by 1860 there were over four million slaves in the country.

Early farms and factories in the North were small enough not to require imported laborers. Quakers and abolitionists found slavery morally offensive as well, although there were some New Englanders who reaped financial fortunes through the importing and selling of slaves in southern ports. White slaves outnumbered blacks until 1700, when sprawling plantations of sugar, rice, tobacco, and indigo demanded huge numbers of workers. After Eli Whitney invented the cotton gin in 1793, the demand for southern cotton skyrocketed. Boats bringing black slaves from Africa were crowded, the price of a quality field hand ranging from $300 to $400.

Once on the plantation, work hours were long and tiring. A few slaves were fortunate enough to work indoors as domestics, but most had to work in fields, spending 14-hour days under a blazing sun. Housing provided by slaveowners was substandard at best, with owners paying more attention to feeding their workers well in order to work them harder. What little pleasure the slaves had came from sharing the folklore and song of their African heritage.

When the U.S. Constitution was adopted in 1787, it prohibited Congress from stopping the slave trade before 1808. In that year, Congress exercised the power extended by the Constitution and forever put an end to the legal importation of slaves. Nonetheless, slaves continued to be smuggled into the country, largely through the efforts of New England traders and southern planters.

As the nation expanded in the early and middle 19th century, Congress found slavery to be a constant problem. Differences were often resolved through concession and com- promise, but such laws offered only tem- porary relief. The North and South drew steadily apart until the Civil War was fought to finally settle the differences. During that conflict, Abraham Lincoln issued the Emanci- pation Proclamation in 1863. It called for the liberation of those slaves held in states still in rebellion. Finally, the 13th Amendment to the Constitution in 1865 freed all slaves within the United States and forbid the institution of slavery for all time.

Largely through the shrewd political maneuvering of Speaker of the House Henry Clay, a compromise was reached prohibiting slavery in all lands north of 36°30′ latitude ex- cept Missouri. People living in lands south of this line could vote their choice (popular sovereignty), but it was assumed such states would select to allow slavery. Thus, when Maine entered the Union as a free state in 1820, Missouri entered as a slave state in 1821.

On the surface, this arrangement seemed to satisfy all concerned. But beneath the outer calm, there were feelings of discontent. It was not long before the astute Buchanan sensed that all were not happy with the Missouri Compromise of 1820. But there were other, more pressing matters calling for his personal attention. He knew and understood the wishes of the people back in his Pennsylvania district, and he would represent them as best he could.

Tariffs, Education, and Other Issues

First of all, Buchanan made certain that tariffs (taxes on imports) were kept high on those foreign imports that competed with goods produced in Pennsylvania. Anyone in Congress who attempted to lower duties on such commodities as molasses, hemp, or iron risked an all-out fight with the gentleman from Lancaster.

Buchanan was equally fierce in his support of public education. Although he cherished the memories of all his own mother had done in teaching him at home during his early years, he recalled the excitement of attending classes at the grammar school in Mercersburg. The idea that young people in the nation might not enjoy similar learning experiences through an educational system open to all troubled him, and he devoted much energy to this cause.

Immigration laws were another issue being discussed in Congress, where some efforts were being made to limit the number of people of certain nationalities from entering the country. Such thinking did not meet with Buchanan's approval. "We should be flattered that so many would be willing to leave their homelands with all the sacrifices that might suggest, and journey across the sea to a new, unknown continent. Surely they come here having heard of our strengths, our opportunities. Are we then to hold up a sign saying 'You are not wanted here'? I think not. We should take all we can take." Remembering his own father's immigration, the man from Lancaster smiled. "Especially the Irish!"

Although a staunch believer in the Union, Buchanan stood firmly behind the idea of states enjoying certain rights within their own boundaries, and individual citizens having a maximum amount of freedom within their own homes. "No person should feel constricted by laws and regulations established by the democratic system in which he lives," Buchanan wrote to a friend. He went on:

> If the federal system of government is going to succeed in America, it must promote a sense of personal worth and opportunity within each of its citizens. To impose restrictions is to return to the tyranny our fathers fought to overthrow. Whether a man be a farmer, a store clerk or a servant to the public, he should be able to turn to his government for protection of his rights and freedoms. That government should stand ready to assist each citizen in achieving all that he can.

Fair Treatment for All

Aware that many members of Congress enjoyed considerable wealth, Buchanan became a special watchdog on behalf of the poor. He still recalled his days in the Pennsylvania legislature, when the battle raged over conscription for military service. There were many in eastern Pennsylvania who could afford to put up the conscription fee, but there were many in the western part of the state who were too poor to do so. Just as it would have been unfair to assess the rich and poor alike at the state level, Buchanan wanted fair treatment for all citizens of the nation.

"I know you'll be looking out for us," wrote one farmer from Buchanan's home district. "I tell my wife that we may not have much else here on the homestead, but we got a good Congressman in Washington named The Honorable James Buchanan." Despite the support of fellow Federalists (a political party waning in numbers and power), a national banking system never did win Buchanan's approval because it favored those with wealth.

Buchanan was also opposed to the government delegating funds to repair the Cumberland Road. Running through Maryland, Pennsylvania, and Virginia, the route had been a federal project before Buchanan arrived in Washington. But when money was requested of Congress to make needed repairs, controversy arose.

Businessmen in Pennsylvania had constructed a private road between Philadelphia and Pittsburgh for which a small toll was charged. No toll was charged on the Cumberland Road, which is exactly what Buchanan wanted in 1822. "Competition in business is only good sense," he asserted, "and should we not encourage the free enterprise system in a democracy?"

Seeking a compromise, Buchanan suggested that the Cumberland Road be turned over to the three states directly involved, but that move was voted down. Ultimately, Buchanan supported a high tariff on any goods brought into Pennsylvania on the Cumberland Road, feeling such an action would protect his state's constituents. Although the passageway remained free and was repaired with federal funds, the people back home felt they had been well served by James Buchanan, Jr. Each time he ran for re-election, he was returned to Congress by substantial margins.

GETTING A POLITICAL EDUCATION

The handsome Buchanan was frequently invited to dinner parties and receptions, often with the matchmaking hopes of some Washington socialite. But more often than not, the unattached bachelor ended up discussing the latest political entanglements with the gentlemen present rather than paying any attention to the single ladies. The passing years did little to erase the sad memories of Ann Coleman, and Buchanan showed little interest in finding a new love.

Instead, his love became politics. From his youth, Buchanan had prided himself on always being ready for whatever the occasion demanded. He carried such traits into his congressional role, often sharing detailed notes that he had prepared with his colleagues about matters brought before the House floor. House Speaker Henry Clay was well aware of Buchanan's devotion to his duties.

The Presidential Election of 1824

The election of 1824 was probably more confusing and exciting than any previous presidential contest. As usual, the members of the House of Representatives gathered in their chamber to select a presidential candidate. The popularity of James Monroe during his two terms of office, from March 1817 to March 1825, was unchallenged. "The Era of Good Feeling" persisted, and those attending the congressional caucus (a closed meeting to select candidates to determine policy) knew that whomever they selected would not have Monroe's national appeal. Nevertheless, they chose William Harris Crawford from Georgia as their presidential candidate.

Because Crawford's selection displeased members of several state legislatures, they claimed they would no longer automatically approve presidential choices made by congressional caucuses. Andrew Jackson was nominated by the Tennessee legislature, while the Massachusetts group tapped John Quincy Adams. Joining Crawford, Jackson, and Adams on the ballot was Henry Clay, chosen by his legislature in Kentucky. Each candidate represented a different faction of the Democratic-Republican Party.

On November 2, 1824, American voters went to the polls. The final results found Jackson with 153,544 of the popular count, Adams with 108,740, Crawford with 47,136, and Clay tallying 46,618. In the electoral college, Jackson received 99 votes; Adams, 84; Crawford, 41; and Clay, 37. Because no candidate received a majority of the electoral votes, the final decision moved to the House of Representatives to choose a President from the three leading contenders.

There was no doubt where Buchanan stood. He had always been impressed with Andrew Jackson, although the two men did not know each other very well. Adams, on the other hand, had frequently taken a strong stand against tariffs in his position as secretary of state during the Monroe administration. Buchanan and other Pennsylvanians felt such taxes were necessary to protect American manufacturers. They hoped Adams would fail in his quest for the White House, but they did not want to leave anything to chance.

Adams Wins

Destined to play a pivotal role in this political drama was Henry Clay. His fourth-place position in the presidential race eliminated him as a candidate, but he had captured 37 electoral votes in the contest. Moreover, as Speaker of the House, where the outcome would be decided, Clay's actions were crucial. Several of Buchanan's friends urged him to visit Jackson in order to find out who would be his choice for secretary of state. If he expressed support for Clay, the House Speaker might do what he could on Jackson's behalf. Reluctantly, Buchanan agreed.

After Buchanan visited Jackson at his lodgings, the two men then walked to the War Department, where Jackson had meetings scheduled. To his eagerly awaiting colleagues, Buchanan's remarks were simple—Jackson had made no decisions regarding his Cabinet should he be elected. Furthermore, he had made no commitments to anyone regarding any positions, nor did he intend to do so.

When the balloting for President began in the House of Representatives, one teller from each of the 24 states was appointed to examine the ballots and cast one vote for whomever his state had selected. The supporters of Henry Clay shifted their votes to John Quincy Adams. Thus, when the final tabulation was made, Adams won the election with 13 votes (Jackson had seven and Crawford had four).

It was a bitter disappointment for Buchanan and his colleagues. And it came as little surprise when Adams named Henry Clay as his secretary of state. Such was Washington politics, a game Buchanan was learning more about every day.

Chapter 5

At the Court of St. Petersburg

As often as he could, Buchanan returned to Mercersburg. His mother's health was failing now that she was in her sixties, and as the eldest son, Buchanan felt it his position to pay her bills and look after her as much as possible. Sometimes it troubled him being in Washington so much of the time, but Elizabeth Speer Buchanan would have none of such talk. "You have far more important matters to take care of there," she admonished him. But in truth, although he enjoyed the political arena with its constant drama, he also welcomed the time spent peacefully with his family. (Buchanan himself suffered from a liver ailment much of his life but seldom complained to those around him.)

A LOST FRIEND

Although Andrew Jackson had failed in his first attempt to be President, everyone knew that he had not permanently given up the quest. It was pleasing to Buchanan to note that he so often agreed with Jackson's political philosophy and took similar sides on numerous issues. The two men often communicated by letter, and the tone of their exchanges reflected a warm regard for each other.

Because of their friendship, it came as a major surprise to Buchanan when, early in 1827, articles suddenly appeared in news periodicals that quoted Jackson as criticizing the Pennsylvania representative. "I know from my own experience," observed Jackson, "that James Buchanan is not to be trusted." The remarks stung Buchanan deeply, for he had considered Jackson to be not only a political ally but a friend as well. Now the newspaper accounts claimed that the purpose of Buchanan's visit to Jackson on that day in 1825 was to secure a Cabinet position for himself, should Jackson be elected. It was nonsense, to be sure, but the accusations left Buchanan devastated.

Again and again, Buchanan had supported Jackson's ideas, always challenging the attempts by John Quincy Adams to expand the reins of federal power and pull them ever tighter. More than almost anyone, Buchanan longed for Jackson to make another try for the presidency. Now this same man accused him of "devious dealing" to reach higher office.

Not only did Jackson's remarks make the Washington newspapers, they made headlines in the *Lancaster Journal,* too. Buchanan answered the charges, denying each one, and suggested that Jackson should become better informed. "For one who clearly seeks the executive rung on the political ladder, and who fancies himself worthy of governing the citizens of this grand nation, it might do well to find better sources of information. Statesmanship demands wiser thinking and more honest expression," Buchanan fired back in writing.

Another Election, Another Win

Despite the personal hurt suffered by Jackson's accusations, Buchanan set about organizing Pennsylvanians for the 1828 presidential election. No longer would a congressional caucus choose the candidate for the nation's highest office; such a method worked contrary to the Constitution, so Jackson supporters claimed. Buchanan agreed. The new policy called for state legislatures to make the nominations.

The results of the change placed Jackson against Adams in the November election. This time, there was no question about the outcome. Jackson and his vice-presidential running mate, John C. Calhoun of South Carolina, received 647,286 popular votes to 508,064 for Adams and his vice-presidential candidate, Richard Rush of Pennsylvania. Of 261 electoral votes, Jackson received 178 to Adams' 83. And once more, James Buchanan was returned to the House of Representatives from his home district in Pennsylvania. He hoped that all of the vicious sniping in the press and the mudslinging that had taken place during the presidential campaign were now in the past.

A FRIENDSHIP RENEWED

As far as Buchanan's relationship with President Jackson was concerned, it appeared that political and personal fences between the two men were mended by November of 1830. At that time, Buchanan's younger brother, George, received a letter from Martin Van Buren, Jackson's secretary of state, stating that George had been appointed district attorney for the Pittsburgh region. Although the letter came from Van Buren, the commission from President Jackson was enclosed.

The new chief executive was not known for making personal apologies, but James Buchanan accepted George's appointment as such. He was not one to hold grudges, particularly against the President of the United States and the leader of his political party. Because Buchanan's political philosophy was so close to that of Jackson and his supporters, he now felt comfortable calling himself "a Democrat."

Judiciary Chairman

Buchanan also felt comfortable, and honored besides, when he was appointed chairman of the House Judiciary Committee. Although a firm advocate of states' rights, particularly in the area of free business enterprise, Buchanan was equally convinced that the Union could only be strengthened by a judicial system that saw each citizen's rights firmly protected. "The Constitution of the United States was written in blood shed by patriotic Americans," the judiciary chairman told other members of the committee, "and we must do everything possible to preserve those freedoms guaranteed within that document."

When a federal judge was impeached (accused of misconduct) for mishandling his authority in a personal feud, Buchanan was personally outraged that anyone vested with so noble a responsibility could damage its image. But as committee chairman, he hid his personal feelings and conducted a fair and impartial review of the case. The impeachment was narrowly defeated, but it served as a warning to all federal judges that they had better keep "their own robes clean."

When an effort was made to abolish a phase of the Judiciary Act of 1789, an act which fortified the national court system, Buchanan again stood up and was counted. He knew the mood of most House members was against too many powers being vested within the Supreme Court (the issue of states' rights versus federal rights was popping up more and more frequently), but Buchanan was determined to protect the strengths of the highest court in the land. His oratory was sincere and at times even fiery, and when the votes were counted, Buchanan's cause won, 138 votes to 51.

A PRESIDENTIAL APPOINTMENT

From his vantage point in the White House, President Jackson kept a careful eye on the House member from Lancaster, Pennsylvania. Despite their earlier falling out, Jackson was more and more convinced that he had indeed been misinformed about Buchanan's intentions during the election of 1824. Certainly such misunderstandings had happened before within the complexities of the Washington political arena. Anyway, Buchanan had more than proven his worth in organizing Pennsylvania in support of Jackson during the 1828 presidential contest.

On another level of political thought, perhaps not quite as pure, Jackson was aware of Buchanan's rising popularity among other Democrats. A bit of such popularity was fine enough, but as President, Jackson enjoyed the unofficial crown as titular head of the party. No challengers to that role were welcome.

It was such political and public evaluation that led Jackson to call in Buchanan and offer him a new role. "I'd like you to consider becoming our American ambassador to Russia," said Jackson. "It would allow you an entirely different spectrum of public service." That much was true, Buchanan agreed. However, it was not truly a "spectrum" he wished to experience. His first reaction was to reject the offer. But Jackson offered convincing argument supporting the idea, then insisted Buchanan mull over his final decision.

A Reluctant Acceptance

It was not an easy choice, and Buchanan had already wrestled with the decision of just how much public service he wanted to give. As a practicing lawyer in Lancaster, he knew he could earn well over $11,000 yearly, a handsome income in 1830. The few legal matters he could handle while an active House member would only bring in about $2,000. It was a considerable difference. Not only that, because his mother was becoming more frail and needed considerable care, Buchanan felt the strong tug of conscience to return home.

The combination of financial and family concerns had caused Buchanan to relinquish his House seat on March 3, 1831. He had even rejected a halfhearted effort by Pennsylvanians to interest him in a vice-presidential role. Buchanan had washed his hands of further service to his country in any kind of official position.

Jackson, however, was not one to give up easily. In Buchanan he sensed a man who thought first of his country and then of himself. When Buchanan again attempted to decline the appointment to Russia—"My place is in Lancaster"— the insistent Jackson countered with, "Your heart is in America." Not without reservations, Buchanan gave in. He would serve his country at the court of St. Petersburg.

Public announcement of the appointment was not immediate because the present minister to Russia, John Randolph, had not yet turned in his resignation. It was only a matter of time, however, because Randolph's health could not tolerate the cold Russian climate. As Buchanan busied himself studying French (the official language of the Russian court), rumors persisted that he might make himself available for the vice-presidency. He denied the rumors emphatically, yet he had been around Washington long enough to know that too much denial brought even more suspicion. "This is a city of wagging tongues," Buchanan wrote home.

Buchanan was happy to return to Lancaster in order to take care of business before departing for Russia. His mother did not want him to go, fearing she would die in his absence, but Buchanan felt that he had to go. (She did die while he was in Russia, plunging him into a deep depression.)

ARRIVAL IN RUSSIA

By April of 1832 Buchanan had finished up business and family matters in Lancaster, obtained his passport and diplomatic instructions at the State Department in Washington, called on the White House for a personal visit with President Jackson, and was ready to depart. An Army officer, John Barry, was appointed as his secretary, and a government employee, Edward Landrick, was to be his valet. They sailed on a Sunday aboard the *Silas Richards,* leaving from New York City and heading for Liverpool, England. New to sea travel, Buchanan took ill almost immediately and spent most of the voyage in his cabin. Nonetheless, after the 25-day journey, the new minister to Russia hosted a dinner party in the captain's honor and led in multiple toasts. Once his health returned, Buchanan enjoyed a two-week holiday in Europe.

By the time Buchanan arrived in St. Petersburg, it was June. He was surprised at the bitter cold, and equally flabbergasted at the brightness of the nights. No candles were required to read in the evenings, even past midnight, and the new ambassador was grateful for every way he could find of saving money. Formal dress was required at all times, and he was obliged to reside in a large villa with stables, horses, a carriage, and multiple servants. It was clear to Buchanan that his annual salary of $9,000 would have to be carefully budgeted.

Buchanan was introduced at the court of Czar Nicholas I immediately, and it did not take long to realize the Russian leader was a man of few words. The Czar's wife, however, was another story. She obviously welcomed any new face, especially one as handsome as Buchanan's, and constantly engaged the new American ambassador in lengthy conversation.

The Czarina showed much interest in the growing friction between the southern and northern states in America.

Russians, as well as other Europeans, wondered if there might be another revolution, this time among the United States. Buchanan did his best to allay their fears, writing home to Jackson, "God forbid that the Union should be in any danger."

Negotiating Treaties

But the problems of America were now thousands of miles away. Buchanan had instructions to pursue a dual course of action regarding treaties. One was to establish a strong commercial trading agreement, while the second was to provide maritime rights of American ships in Russian waters. Count Nesselrode, the Russian foreign minister, seemed to be in favor of the two treaties. However, neither the Russian minister of finance, Count Cancrene, nor Russian minister to the United States, Baron Krudener, appeared eager to extend any relationships.

Buchanan grew impatient with having to pamper and pacify the Russian officials, but he restrained himself from making any public declaration of his frustration. He also wearied of the oppressive atmosphere at the court, writing to Jackson, "Here there is no freedom of the press, no public opinion, and but little political conversation and that much guarded. In short, we live in the calm of despotism."

Avoiding Confrontations

Within that "calm," Buchanan learned to function in a far different manner than he had in the political arena of the United States. In America, it was possible to arouse public opinion on one side of an issue or another and use that support for political maneuvering. None of that was possible in Russia. There was a ruling aristocracy and serfs (peasants) "wholly unfit to take any share in the government, and it is doubtless the policy of the Emperor and nobles to keep them in this state of ignorance," Buchanan noted. As to a middle class, there simply was none in Russia.

If Buchanan hoped to achieve his goals in St. Petersburg, there would be no reaching out to the people for help. His fellow Americans were too far away to lend assistance, and the peasants of Russia knew nothing of how their government functioned. Buchanan zeroed in on Count Nesselrode while trying to avoid any negative confrontations with other Russian officials.

Buchanan managed to make headway, partly because of his own personal appeal and partly because Nesselrode did not consider the United States a major power. In a treaty for expanding commercial trade, Russia would certainly be able to supply America with far more goods of any kind than the other way around.

As for the maritime treaty, everything was going smoothly until the American press criticized Russia for its behavior with its neighbor Poland. The Czar and others took the American ambassador to task for such criticism. Buchanan tried to explain that the government in the United States did not control the press—that it was free to say what it pleased—but his voice was not heard.

Return Home

Realizing there was no hope for the maritime treaty and fearing he would be forgotten politically by supporters back in the United States, Buchanan respectfully asked to be relieved of his position. After being granted permission to leave late in the summer of 1833, Buchanan made his final appearance at the court of Czar Nicholas. Known for his strict composure in public, the Russian leader nonetheless embraced Buchanan, telling him to relay his gratitude to President Jackson. "Please have your leader send us another minister exactly like yourself," the Czar said. Smiling, Buchanan walked proudly from the room.

Chapter 6
Serving in the Senate

James Buchanan knew he had missed life in the United States, but he had no idea just how much until he returned. "One can almost smell freedom in the air," he told President Jackson during the retired diplomat's visit to the White House upon his return.

The Pennsylvania surroundings were even more appreciated, as Buchanan found himself welcomed back to the Lancaster family and friends he had missed so much. Hosts and hostesses invited him to cheerful social gatherings where he shared stories of life in Russia. Few were interested in the political events at St. Petersburg, which was just as well because they would have obtained no secrets from the guest of honor. Buchanan was quite aware of the duties and responsibilities of his position even after it had officially ended, and he entertained his audiences only with tales of Russian fashions, foods, and culture.

Ann Coleman's family had left Lancaster, and when Buchanan heard their home was for sale, he bought it. The days of his earlier romance with Ann were not forgotten, but the passage of time had softened the sadness. He entertained his brothers and sisters with their children, a task eased with the help of a young housekeeper. "Uncle Jim" was a family favorite, often bragged about for his personal association with President Jackson and other political figures. Buchanan rekindled his law practice, too, being pleased when many former clients returned to seek his counsel.

BACK TO WASHINGTON

Although the people of the Lancaster community were glad to have Buchanan back among them, most were certain he would not stay for long. After spending so much time in Washington and St. Petersburg, surely he would find life dull in the small Pennsylvania town. Buchanan simply laughed when such remarks were made in his presence, but he had to admit that time weighed heavy on his hands.

Late in December of 1834, U.S. Senator Wilkins of Pennsylvania was appointed to fill Buchanan's former position in Russia. State legislators approached Buchanan about taking Wilkins' spot in the Senate. Happily, Buchanan returned to Washington and immediately became caught up in the political whirl.

The National Bank Issue—Again

In a sense, Buchanan felt that he had never left Washington, for once again the argument raged over the rechartering of the national bank. However, because the money in the federal coffers was increasing all the time, this seemed to compound the issue.

President Jackson never had accepted the "monster corporation" that was the national bank, and led the Democratic opposition to it with all the old generalmanship skills he could muster. His Vice-President, Martin Van Buren, supported the concept of a federal bank. But as a New Yorker, Van Buren would have preferred to have the funds kept in his state rather than in Pennsylvania, where the national bank was located. Naturally, Buchanan's constituents wanted the money to stay in Pennsylvania. To Jackson, the location of the bank was secondary to its existence. Jackson led the opposition in the face of such forceful bank supporters as John C. Calhoun, Henry Clay, and Daniel Webster.

Gaining Notice

Buchanan quickly took Jackson's side, yet his past experiences in Washington had taught him the game of politics well. He also kept on Van Buren's good side, recognizing that the Vice-President would be the most likely successor to Jackson in the White House.

When a nasty dispute between America and France regarding financial claims broke out in the Senate, Buchanan used the diplomatic skills he had acquired during his stint as ambassador to Russia. He understood the depth and breadth of foreign relations, had known some of the officials personally, and managed to ease much of the strain between the two countries. Each day found Buchanan winning more and more notice within the Democratic Party.

As the fires heated up for the presidential election of 1836, Van Buren was clearly the Democratic Party choice, while the opposition had formed a party called the Whigs. General William Henry Harrison was the presidential candidate selected by the Whig Party, but on election day, Americans gave Van Buren a resounding victory. At the same time, the voters of Pennsylvania returned Buchanan to the Senate for a full six-year term. Since he had done so much in organizing Pennsylvanians for Van Buren, Buchanan returned to Washington basking in the glow of the White House.

More Bank Problems

Problems were not long in coming. As a final executive action, Jackson signed legislation to remove all government money in the federal bank and redeposit it in state banks. Paper money was then printed by the state banks, using the federal funds on deposit to back up the paper money. Inflation (the over-availability of money, causing prices to rise) set in, forcing Jackson to require that federal land must be purchased with gold or silver. This managed to curb inflation, but Americans still remained uncertain about money values and even job security. Foreign countries also questioned the economic stability of the United States, and commercial trade diminished. Van Buren and the 25th Congress, both sworn in on March 4, 1837, grappled with such problems throughout the spring and summer. In October, ten million dollars in Treasury notes were issued, hoping to squelch the multitude of economic problems known as the Panic of 1837. The turmoil subsided somewhat, but not enough to enable Van Buren to win a second term in the White House. One of Van Buren's final acts during his administration was to oversee the creation of an independent Treasury system. This system largely originated from Buchanan's suggestion that subtreasuries be established in New York, Boston, Charleston, and St. Louis.

GROWING VOICES AGAINST SLAVERY

The mood of the country was changing. There was a restlessness with the way things had been combined with a feeling of exploration and discovery. Caught up in the fever, more pioneers headed west. Others, content to stay where they were, looked around and saw conditions that they did not like. Slavery was one such condition.

Long an institution in the country, slavery had never before been as critically analyzed and discussed. Voices of those wanting the practice abolished, called abolitionists, rose in criticism, and their voices carried into Congress. As a political party, the newly formed Whigs, bolstered by ever-growing numbers, supported the abolitionist cause.

While personally detesting slavery himself, Buchanan stood firm on the side of the Constitution, declaring often and publicly, "A man has the right to own property, and while his slaves be considered his property, no government should take away such property." It was Buchanan's hope that slaveowners might see their way toward freeing their slaves on their own.

Most of Buchanan's fellow Pennsylvanians and other northern politicians laughed at such a notion. But Buchanan felt a special closeness to southerners. He was Scotch-Irish, just as many of them were. Southerners, like himself, prided themselves on dress and manners, a certain style of grace and elegance. Social amenities were important to southerners and Buchanan, particularly since he had served in the diplomatic corps abroad. Northerners seemed to put little value on such things, often snickering at Buchanan's references to "the ladies and gentlemen of the South."

Stand on Slavery

In 1836 Buchanan took his stand on slavery to the floor of the Senate, and his position on the issue wavered little over the years that followed. He pointed out that slavery had existed in the country before the Union was formed or the Constitution adopted. In establishing the federal government, representatives of the individual states had not given that government any right to interfere with their way of life or with their property rights.

When the Pennsylvania Society for the Abolition of Slavery had brought up the issue in 1790, the U.S. House of Representatives resolved "That Congress have no authority to interfere in the emancipation of slaves, or in the treatment of them within any of the states; it remaining with the several states alone to provide any regulations therein, which humanity and true policy may require." As Buchanan saw the matter, the southern states had entered the Union with an understanding that slavery was acceptable; there was no legal and just way in which the federal government could abolish it.

Despite Buchanan's stand on the slavery matter itself, he defended the right of citizens to bring petitions against it. "Any citizen of our land, our democracy, shall always enjoy the freedom of circulating petitions in order to gain support for whatever cause he wishes," said Buchanan.

No doubt, Buchanan recalled his service in Russia, where he had witnessed a governmental system totally removed from input by the citizens. He wanted none of that. Yet he looked with disdain on the emotional abolitionists, feeling such "fanatics" caused slaveowners to "tighten the reins of authority over their slaves" in order to enforce strict discipline.

THE WHIGS TAKE OVER

With the election of 1840, Democrats rallied around their incumbent leader, President Martin Van Buren. Buchanan had been offered a spot in the next Cabinet, but he did not wish to become Attorney General should Van Buren win. The fact was that Buchanan was quite content in the Senate, never actually leading a cause or pushing a personal issue, but rather lending support and sharing his opinions.

The Whigs, constantly growing in strength, once again

picked William Henry Harrison to lead their ticket. Buchanan, having been elected to the Senate three years before, had another three years before he had to campaign again, so he returned to Pennsylvania to speak on behalf of Van Buren. Americans, however, associated Van Buren with the Panic of 1837. He was also often identified with handing out jobs based on political reward (patronage) rather than merit.

Although Harrison had no governmental service other than military, he was swept into office by the voters. Sworn in on March 3, 1841, he died only 32 days later, apparently of pneumonia and its complications. The mantle of leadership passed swiftly to Vice-President John Tyler.

Presidents Tyler and Polk

On the surface, it would appear that the Whig Party had a firm control on the government of the United States, boasting a President and majorities in both the Senate and the House of Representatives. But within months, "Honest John" Tyler shocked his political colleagues by publicly opposing the establishment of a national bank through a veto of congressional legislation. Henry Clay and other Whig leaders were furious, but they could not override Tyler's veto. Buchanan was delighted at the discontent within the opposing ranks and eagerly took on Clay himself over various financial issues.

Before long, Tyler realized his own party had disowned him, and the chief executive worked to solidify relations with the Democrats. But other than a treaty defining the Maine-Canada boundary, a peace-commerce treaty with China, and the annexation of Texas, the Tyler years slipped by with little accomplishment.

In the meantime, Buchanan worked actively within the Senate, patching up differences among fellow Democrats and keeping the wheels of government rolling smoothly. Seldom did he seek any spotlight, satisfied instead to be a good team worker. "No one may remember that I even served this body," he once wrote about his time in the Senate, "but I would hope that the country is better for that service."

As the presidential election of 1844 approached, it was clear the Whigs would have nothing more to do with Tyler, returning to their party head, Henry Clay. Buchanan hoped that he might be asked to carry the Democratic banner. Instead, however, his colleagues turned to James Knox Polk.

A longtime member of the House of Representatives, Polk had served the Democratic Party faithfully. In 1839, although he would have preferred to remain in Washington, Polk was persuaded to run for governor of Tennessee. Elected once, he failed in two subsequent tries.

Polk had been a "dark horse" at the Democratic convention in 1844 until Buchanan withdrew his own name as momentum grew on Polk's behalf. Back to Pennsylvania Buchanan went, campaigning for his third Senate term and also speaking out for Polk. Both men won in the November elections, with Pennsylvania displaying a strong Democratic vote. But as James Buchanan made plans for another six years in the Senate, other plans were being made that would completely alter the future of the man from Lancaster.

Chapter 7

Clouds of War

Again James Buchanan read the letter he held in his hands. It was a formal request from President-elect James Polk to serve as secretary of state in his administration. Certainly the letter had not come as a complete surprise. Rumors of possible Polk appointees had circulated even before the election itself. Once the former governor of Tennessee was elected, his aides had called on Buchanan both in Lancaster and in Washington. His opinions were asked, his attitudes analyzed. His public record in the House and the Senate were well known, but it was important to review his thoughts and feelings.

After all, the role of secretary of state was no menial position in a President's administration. It was a key Cabinet appointment, perhaps the most crucial of all. As Buchanan studied the invitation, he was a happy man indeed. Polk already knew the invitation would be accepted—what he did not know was how proud Buchanan felt at being asked.

SECRETARY OF STATE

The previous years had been full of political squabbling, pitting the Whigs against their own President. And the Democrats were finding it difficult to determine whether the opposition was in the White House or in governmental chambers with them. With the election of Polk, there was hope that political fences could be mended and the business of building a bigger, stronger nation could continue.

In the background, rumblings of the slavery issue could be heard. But Polk had run on a platform of expansion, and Americans were caught up in a desire for growth, perhaps of acquiring the Oregon Territory from Great Britain and the California Territory from Mexico. It was a time for dreaming that the United States could become the richest and grandest country in the world. Anything was possible with vision and hard work.

But Polk's invitation to Buchanan to join the Cabinet was not unconditional. The new President insisted that his team be devoted to the needs of the nation, and that personal political goals be totally set aside so as not to interfere with their service. Polk himself had pledged to serve but one term in office. Should anyone within the Cabinet have any notions about running for President in 1848, Polk wanted that person out by immediate resignation.

A Potential Candidate

Although Buchanan had yet to feel strongly about being a presidential candidate in 1848, others had broached the possibility to him. And he had even received a few delegate votes at the 1844 Democratic convention. Perhaps every individual with a slight case of political fever at some point dreams of someday rising to the top, but for most it is just a fleeting thought. Nonetheless, Buchanan jotted a short, honest reply to Polk, making his position clear:

> I do not know that I shall ever desire to be a candidate
> for the Presidency. Most certainly I never yet strongly felt
> such an indication, and I have been willing and should at this

moment be willing to accept a station which would, in my estimation of what is proper, deprive me of any prospect of reaching that office. Still, I could not, and would not, accept the high and honorable office to which you have called me at the expense of self-ostracism. My friends would unanimously condemn me were I to pursue this course. I cannot proclaim to the world that in no contingency shall I be a candidate for the Presidency in 1848.

The cards were on the table. If Polk wanted Buchanan to serve in his Cabinet, it would be with the understanding that the gentleman from Lancaster would leave open the doors to the future. Polk respected such frankness and honesty; Buchanan became secretary of state.

Little Time to Prepare

There was little time for Buchanan to become acclimated to his new position. Even before the election, Congress had approved statehood for Texas. But it was not all that simple. Mexico had never recognized the independence of Texas, and there was also disagreement over the boundary between Texas and Mexico. Not only that, abolitionists raised their voices in fear that Texas would join the Union as a slave state.

Polk had a ready-made solution for the last concern. The acquisition of Oregon and its admission to the Union as a free state would appease the abolitionists, or so he hoped. "However, the expansion of this great nation shall not depend upon the political thinking of a group of individuals, including and especially the President of the United States," Polk asserted.

As secretary of state, James Buchanan had his work cut out for him. From the outset, he knew the task would not be an easy one. Whereas he was known for slow, deliberate action based on detailed analysis, his chief was more inclined toward quick, sweeping movements and an impatience with anyone or anything that would impede progress as he saw it. Yes, it would be a challenge for both men.

Oregon and Texas

As far as the Oregon Territory was concerned, there had been little governmental action concerning it since 1827. The territory was still largely unknown land, but an influx of American settlers eager to farm demanded further action. Polk selected the 49th parallel as a dividing line between the territory and Canada. When Great Britain refused such a boundary, Polk pushed even further, demanding that latitude 54°40' be the boundary. "And if they do not agree, we shall cut off communications with them," snapped the President. As a trained and experienced diplomat, such an attitude toward negotiations shocked Buchanan. He felt that avenues of communications should be kept open at all costs.

There was also the heated controversy over Texas. In that case, Buchanan had no real opportunity to negotiate a peaceful settlement because all diplomatic relations with Mexico ended in March of 1845, the same month Polk took power. Leaders from Texas turned to the United States government to safeguard them as they prepared to become a state. In December, 1845, Texas became the 28th state of the Union.

WAR WITH MEXICO

As the Mexican armies gathered for war, Buchanan put his knowledge of diplomacy into play. It was essential, he told Polk, that Mexico appear to be the aggressor if fighting broke out. This was because there were foreign powers that already thought the United States seemed to be reaching too far and too fast in acquiring new lands. (Indeed, Polk not only hoped to bring Texas into the Union, but New Mexico and California as well!) It was essential that the nation show its strength if Mexico attacked, but it was equally important not to fire the first shot in any kind of military encounter.

Polk found it difficult restraining his top generals, just as the generals found it challenging to hold back their men as they gathered along the Mexico-Texas border. Late in April of 1846, a scouting party under the supervision of General Zachary Taylor was viciously attacked by some 1,600 Mexican soldiers led by General Anastasio Torrejon. "Hostilities may now be considered as commenced," Taylor wrote to Polk. Indeed the Mexican-American War was on!

Settling the Oregon Dispute

There was nothing Buchanan could do about the southwestern boundary of the nation during the period of active military combat between the United States and Mexico. But he had no intention of remaining inactive in his position as secretary as state. While U.S. generals Taylor and Winfield Scott were leading Americans to military victories in Mexico, Buchanan was fighting a bureaucratic conflict with the British minister to the United States, Richard Pakenham, over settlement of the Oregon dispute.

There could be little concession on the Oregon issue by the United States because President Polk had already issued numerous public statements supporting the Manifest Destiny policy of stretching the nation's borders from the Atlantic Ocean to the Pacific Ocean. Polk's manner of declaring every move to the world was in direct conflict with Buchanan's own diplomacy, which was based on quiet, careful negotiations between countries. But James Knox Polk was President of the United States, and no one knew that better than James

Buchanan. Polk had definite ideas regarding foreign policy and expected his secretary of state to carry out his wishes.

While the interest of most Americans focused on the on-going war with Mexico, Buchanan continued to work quietly with Pakenham in an effort to settle the Oregon question. Polk was totally caught up in the southwestern conflict and wanted to give it his full concentration. When Great Britain offered to settle the Oregon boundary at the 49th parallel, Polk told Buchanan to let the matter be settled in the Senate. The senators, too, were more caught up in the business of fighting a war, therefore the matter flowed quite smoothly. On June 15, 1846, a treaty was concluded with Great Britain that established the Oregon Territory boundary at the 49th parallel.

Interest in the Supreme Court

As President, Polk was also empowered to appoint members of the Supreme Court. Early in 1846, Buchanan confided in Louis McLane, the American minister in London, a secret he had held for some time. He wrote:

> I have for years been anxious to obtain a seat on the bench of the Supreme Court. This has been several times within my power; but circumstances have always prevented me from accepting the offered boon. I cannot desert the President, at the present moment, against his protestations. If the Oregon question should not be speedily settled, the vacancy must be filled; and then farewell to my wishes.

Buchanan's interest in a Supreme Court position was hardly a surprise, for despite his extended service in the House and the Senate, it was always the law that held his interest most. He knew every word of the Constitution by heart and was always willing to offer his learned opinion of each phrase, every idea.

After the Oregon Territory boundary had been settled, Buchanan made his interest in the Supreme Court position more public. He won quick support from among those who knew he would make a good judge, some support from those who wanted someone else in his position in the Cabinet, and no support at all from the one who mattered most — James Knox Polk. However, Polk's rejection was not based on negative feeling. Quite the contrary. Polk emphasized his personal need for a man of Buchanan's experience as secretary of state while hostilities with Mexico still existed. Reluctantly, Buchanan agreed. It was not his nature to turn away from what he considered a call to duty.

Ending the War

But as the war against Mexico passed from months into years, Buchanan became more and more restless. If only there were some opportunity to meet with Mexican officials, to discuss differences, to negotiate agreements. There was none of that, only the news of one battle after another being fought. Monterey, Buena Vista, Vera Cruz, Cerro Gordo — each conflict seemed to indicate that the Americans were gaining more and more strength. As 1846 and 1847 slipped by, talk of a U.S. victory grew increasingly louder.

Finally, in September of 1847, General Winfield Scott led American soldiers in the capture of Mexico City, signaling that the war was rapidly coming to an end. Buchanan helped in putting together a treaty of surrender, even managing to calm down his own President, who wanted all of Mexico as the victor's prize. Instead, Buchanan managed to design a treaty that would give the United States not only Texas, but California and other southwestern territories as well. Mexico was given 15 million dollars in exchange for the land, a payment Polk did not like but which was looked upon with

In 1848, while completing his duties as secretary of state in the administration of President James Polk, Buchanan purchased this estate outside of Lancaster, Pennsylvania. He called the place "Wheatland." (Library of Congress.)

considerable favor by many foreign countries as a noble gesture by the United States.

WHEATLAND

After the treaty with Mexico was signed on February 2, 1848, Buchanan was then freed from many of the most difficult duties of his position. He celebrated by returning to Lancaster, where he purchased a new home, about a mile and a half outside of town.

"Wheatland," as Buchanan called his new residence, boasted a three-story, red brick house, a small stable, and a barn surrounded by a white fence on 22 acres of rolling meadows. It had served as the summer residence of a Philadelphia businessman. Someone not knowing better might have thought that Wheatland was a bit large for a bachelor, but Buchanan had inherited the supervision of numerous nieces and nephews who had lost both of their own parents. "For a bachelor, I have a remarkably big family," he often joked.

In May 1848, Buchanan took a major interest in the Democratic National Convention held in Baltimore. He hoped his political colleagues might remember his many years of public service, transforming that appreciation into a nomination for the presidency. How many other aspirants could claim 10 years of experience in the House of Representatives, two years of diplomatic service abroad, over 10 years serving in the Senate, and four years as secretary of state? If asked to be a presidential candidate, James Buchanan stood ready, even eager.

But it was not to be. The convention delegates chose Senator Lewis Cass of Michigan to lead their ticket. Buchanan had been the second choice of those attending the convention, but it was little consolation. The man from Lancaster had hoped for the big prize.

Chapter 8

The Squire of Lancaster

Fresh out of a military conflict in Mexico, Americans found themselves embroiled in another kind of battle, this one of a political nature. Two weeks after the Democrats tapped Lewis Cass to carry their banner in the 1848 election, the Whigs gathered in Philadelphia and selected General Zachary Taylor to run as their presidential candidate. A career Army man, Taylor lacked any political experience or expertise. "So much the better!" more than one cynical American was heard to declare. Moreover, he had never even voted in an election because of constantly moving from one military post to another.

Then, in August, a contingent of antislavery Democrats met in Buffalo, New York, and formed the Free Soil Party. They promptly nominated former President Martin Van Buren as their candidate. More than once, James Buchanan, quietly sipping wine on the front porch of Wheatland, would chuckle as stories of the political goings-on were carried to him by friends.

On November 7, 1848, the voters made their choice. They rewarded their old military hero, Zachary Taylor, with the top office in the land. Cass came in a respectable second, while Van Buren trailed dismally behind. Following Taylor's victory, Buchanan remarked to a confidant that he was feeling a bit sorry for himself because Americans, especially those within his own party, did not seem to appreciate experience. But he felt especially sorry for his political adversary, Henry Clay. "Tried five times to be a candidate, and didn't make it once. Heard he lost his son in the Mexico fighting, too." Buchanan turned to watch his young relatives at play as he spoke. "I may be more blessed than I think."

DAYS AT WHEATLAND

People in the southeastern towns and farms of Pennsylvania dubbed Buchanan the "Squire of Lancaster" as they watched the tall, white-haired gentleman ride by in his carriage or stroll around his Wheatland estate. He was always nattily dressed, not given to styles as they came and went, but attired formally and with the best of social manners. He spoke with equal interest to a Lancaster storeowner as he did to a carriage boy, and he was known to pay generously for work done around his home. Visitors came frequently to his dinner table, often sharing giant helpings of sauerkraut and mashed potatoes. In time, his own vests began to stretch a bit as he put on weight, but he seemed little concerned about his health.

What *did* concern Buchanan was the political world around him and even farther away in Washington. Leading Democrats often went out of their way to call on Buchanan at Wheatland. They were impressed at how well informed he continued to be, although he was officially far removed from any political activity. Buchanan read every news periodical he came upon, wrote numerous letters, and was an astute interrogator of those politicians who came visiting.

In July of 1850 President Zachary Taylor died after serv-

Northern newspapers attacked the Fugitive Slave Law, which was passed as part of the Compromise of 1850. The law said that citizens living in free states had to help catch and return runaway slaves or else be fined and sent to prison. (Library of Congress.)

ing only 16 months in office. He was succeeded by Vice-President Millard Fillmore. "Taylor had no political experience, and Fillmore next to none," Buchanan observed. "But I *do* believe that our new President is, at least, aware of his own limitations." (A caustic but true observation—when Fillmore was once offered an honorary university degree, he refused it. "I had not the advantage of a classical education," Fillmore admitted, "and no man should, in my judgment, accept a degree he cannot read.")

The Compromise of 1850

Also in 1850, a historic slavery compromise was passed. Upon applying for admission to the Union, California declared itself a free state, no slaves allowed. Would the other territories so recently acquired through the Mexican conflict also choose to enter the Union as free states? Senator John C. Calhoun of South Carolina and other southern leaders thought so, and it had taken the best efforts of Senators Henry Clay of Kentucky and Daniel Webster of Massachusetts to put together an agreement appeasing all parties.

When the Senate debate ended, the Compromise of 1850 admitted California as a free state, slave trading in Washington, D.C., was outlawed, while the New Mexico and Utah territories were organized and given permission to vote on whether to be free or slave. Also, southerners were given a new law that would help them recapture fugitive slaves.

Although Buchanan accepted the Compromise of 1850, he felt Congress should have allowed the boundaries set by the Missouri Compromise to extend to California. He also felt Congress was letting voters decide issues that were really up to Congress. Once again, it was strict adherence to the Constitution that dictated his thinking.

Disappointed Again

As the election of 1852 neared, Buchanan thought once more about his chances of being the presidential candidate for the Democratic Party. There was no doubt that Fillmore hoped to achieve the office in his own right, but it was equally certain that his fellow Whigs had no intention of granting that favor. They had put up a hero general in Zachary Taylor in 1848, and unfortunately he had died. But they had not exhausted their list of Army generals. There was no secret that another hero of the Mexican-American War, General Winfield Scott, dubbed "Old Fuss and Feathers" by his fellow soldiers, wanted to run for the office.

From everything he had read and heard, Buchanan determined that his most serious competition would again be Lewis Cass, who was already spouting, "I know I can win *this* time" talk to anyone who would listen. As the Democrats convened for their national convention the first week in June of 1852, Buchanan sorely hoped and prayed the news would be delivered to Wheatland that he had been chosen.

Once again, however, Buchanan felt the pangs of disappointment. But it was not Lewis Cass who emerged as the Democratic candidate at the end of the convention in Baltimore. It was a "dark horse" candidate named Franklin Pierce from New Hampshire. A former member of the U.S. House and Senate, Pierce had also served in the Mexican-American War. But he was hardly considered a presidential prospect. In fact, at the convention, he was not nominated until the 49th ballot, when he received 283 of the 289 votes cast. Cass came in second, while Buchanan ran third.

Despite the disappointment of again not being elected, Buchanan had grown to appreciate the quiet and serenity of Wheatland. "There is a peacefulness here that few men enjoy in this world," he wrote to a friend in Washington. "Naturally, there is a joy to the excitement of government, but the longer that I am away from such activities, the more I have come to appreciate those of my own community. I am not certain anything could bring me back."

MINISTER TO GREAT BRITAIN

Nonetheless, Buchanan soon was given that opportunity. One of Pierce's first acts as President was to ask Buchanan to serve as the U.S. minister to Great Britain. There were many within the Democratic Party who urged Pierce to appoint Buchanan as secretary of state, but Pierce had made a pledge that he was not going to appoint to his Cabinet anyone who had served in the Cabinet of another President.

Buchanan was hesitant about accepting the appointment. He had grown quite accustomed to the life at Wheatland, and he hoped to write a book about the Polk administration while he still possessed "the clear vision and memory to do so." At age 62, he questioned whether there were not younger men who were better suited for the job. After all, whether he would spend more time in Washington or London, there would still be much travel between the two cities. In addition, with Great Britain fighting a war in the Crimea, was there really a necessity for a trained American diplomat in London? Major attention by the British would be focused elsewhere.

Pierce stood firm with his request, however, appealing to Buchanan's role as an elder statesman. Not only did Pierce appear to want Buchanan's help overseas, but the new President obviously wished counsel concerning other appointments at home and abroad. At 48 years of age, Pierce was not only the youngest U.S. President ever to be elected, he was also the first President to be born in the 19th century. He seemed even younger than his years, and Buchanan felt an almost fatherly affection toward the man. "I have not denied a request of my country before," Buchanan told Pierce, "and I shall not begin to do so now. I will accept your appointment."

Appointment Confirmed

In truth, it was not all that simple. It was necessary for the Senate to confirm the appointment. But the Senate had been adjourned, and Buchanan was official only in Pierce's mind. This was certainly not enough to satisfy Buchanan, and he insisted on a special calling of a Senate quorum before he would begin his duties. The quorum was called and the nomination confirmed.

As Buchanan prepared to leave for London, he went to meetings at the State Department to learn specifically about his assignment. The new secretary of state, William Marcy of New York, was a breed apart from Buchanan, and the gentleman from Lancaster soon realized it would take all of his diplomatic skills to deal with his own immediate superior. Marcy's informal manner of handling his diplomats and his loose style of directing their actions annoyed the more sedate and formal Buchanan. Nevertheless, he held his tongue, eager to sail for London, where his true mission was.

Buchanan's tasks in England were threefold: to execute commercial trade agreements between the two nations, with appropriate tariffs; to secure an understanding regarding ocean fisheries; and to stabilize British-American relations in Latin America. The last chore demanded ultimate tact because the "stabilizing" was basically an effort to remove British influence and occupation from the area.

Matters of Delicacy

But before he could become involved in the true purpose of his appointment, Buchanan found himself caught up in some bothersome trivial matters. He had to answer the requests of American tourists stopping in London and needing passports. Then, a directive was issued by Marcy that threatened to cause controversy. It called for heads of the U.S. diplomatic corps to appear at their respective courts "in the simple dress of an American citizen."

"You would look like one of the Queen's butlers!" snapped the manager of the British court. "It would be insulting to Her Majesty."

Buchanan pondered the situation, recognizing he was in service to one nation and obligated to respect another. In February of 1854, when Queen Victoria opened Parliament, a circular was distributed stating that "No one can be admitted into the Diplomatic Tribune, or in the body of the House, but in full court dress." Because obeying the Queen's directive would not be in compliance with his own orders, Buchanan did not attend. But his absence created quite a stir, some suggesting that the United States had openly insulted the Queen.

Frustrated with the whole state of affairs and anxious to actively pursue his mission, Buchanan came up with a brilliant compromise when he attended court. In addition to a full-dress suit, including a black coat with white vest and cravat, black pantaloons, and dress boots, he also wore a plain, black-handled, black-hilted dress sword. The sword was obviously an open mark of respect for the Queen, which she duly noted, and the tension subsided.

In an equally successful move, Buchanan invited his niece, Harriet Lane, to join him in London. At age 23, Harriet soon became an accomplished hostess, a sparkling conversationalist, and seemingly interested in all of her uncle's activities. To Buchanan's staid and formal manner, she added zest and spice. Queen Victoria was quite taken with young Harriet, who twirled lightly around the dance floor with Prince Albert, the Queen's husband, at one royal ball. "For-

Buchanan's absence at the official opening of British Parliament in 1854 by Queen Victoria caused a minor diplomatic flap. As a foreign minister, he became caught in the middle of conflicting orders between his own superiors and officials of the Royal Court. (Library of Congress.)

eign diplomacy has never been easy," Buchanan wrote home, "but my young niece has lifted a bit of the burden."

Maintaining the Status Quo

Although Harriet's presence proved delightful to the Queen and to all British subjects who met her, it did little to make Buchanan's official duties any easier. With their attention directed to Crimean battlefields and overcoming a powerful Russian adversary, British officials were not in a mood to expand commercial trade agreements, and the care and well being of fisheries aroused mediocre interest at best.

But certainly Buchanan's actions at least maintained the status quo (current state of affairs), and he could not be faulted for his efforts. He recalled that during Polk's administration he had felt like a "galley slave" while he took orders as secretary of state. Now, as minister to Great Britain, the feeling was similar.

Back home in the United States, President Pierce's attention was hardly focused on England. The slavery issue was catching fire, with proslavery forces in the Kansas legislature demanding admission to the Union as a slave state, but the people of Kansas wanting to be admitted as a free state. Blood had already been spilled in Kansas over the issue, and more seemed sure to follow. Buchanan was just as glad to be out of the country, but he had no idea how much that factor would prove advantageous to him later.

The Ostend Manifesto

A scorecard of Buchanan's ministry in Great Britain would show that he added a few minor commercial trade agreements, and he saw to it that Americans could continue to safely operate their fisheries, especially in the Atlantic. He also found that England had no interest in adding to its possessions in Latin America.

However, Buchanan's efforts to acquire Cuba from Spain did raise a few eyebrows. Certainly the mood of America was toward expansion, and the "Ostend Manifesto," which Buchanan put together with his fellow foreign ministers in France and Spain, reflected that mood exactly. Not only did the diplomatic trio suggest the purchase of Cuba from Spain, but asserted that if Spain chose not to sell, America would "be justified in wresting" Cuba from its owners.

When word reached the United States of the proposal, it was immediately denounced by the antislavery northerners. The ministers to France and Spain were both southerners, well known for their proslavery stance, and Buchanan himself had always shown much warmth toward the southern way of life. Obviously, the effort to acquire Cuba was merely to expand the boundaries of slavery.

The negative response Buchanan received to the Ostend Manifesto, particularly from some of his personal friends and colleagues in Pennsylvania, was especially disheartening. He declared that he was ready to come home, that he had accomplished everything in England within his power.

ELECTION TIME

Surprisingly, Buchanan's absence from the country improved his chances of winning the nomination to be the Democratic presidential candidate in June of 1856. His two leading challengers, the incumbent, President Pierce, and Senator Stephen A. Douglas of Illinois, had taken much abuse for their proslavery stance in the "bleeding Kansas" turmoil. The Whig Party was badly splintered.

As the Democrats convened in Cincinnati to select their

candidate for the November election, most delegates remembered James Buchanan as having served their party long and well. Untainted by the slavery issue (the Ostend Manifesto was not enough to seriously hurt him in the North, while the South applauded his efforts), Buchanan won his party's endorsement. Two weeks later, the Republicans chose John C. Fremont of California to lead their campaign. A third party, officially known as the American Party, but nicknamed "the Know Nothings," selected former President Millard Fillmore to champion their cause. (The unusual label "Know Nothing" originated because members of the party who were asked about it said, "I know nothing." The party died in 1856.)

The Campaign and Slavery

The Republican Party platform (position on issues) on which Fremont ran flatly opposed slavery. Buchanan campaigned on a firm promise to preserve the Union. "I am not friendly to slavery in the abstract," he declared. "But the rights of the South, under our constitutional compact, are as much entitled to protection as those of any other portion of the Union."

At times, Buchanan's feelings became even more eloquent, almost lyrical:

> The night is departing, and the roseate and propitious morn now breaking upon us promises a long day of peace and prosperity for our country. To secure this, all we of the North have to do is to permit our southern neighbors to manage their own domestic affairs, as they permit us to manage ours. It is merely to adopt the golden rule, and do unto them as we would they should do unto us, in the like circumstances. All they ask from us is simply to let them alone.

Never did James Buchanan understand, as he ran for the highest office of the nation, how there could be such con-

At the Democratic National Convention of 1856 held in Cincinnati, Ohio, James Buchanan saw a longtime wish realized—he was nominated by his party to be its candidate for President. (Library of Congress.)

fusion, such emotional furor, over the slavery issue. The Constitution of the land was the ultimate law, with Buchanan stating, "I consider it to employ the expressive language of the day, as a 'finality'—a fixed fact—a most important enactment of the law, the agitation or disturbance of which could do no possible good, but might produce much positive evil."

Throughout the late summer months and early autumn, support grew stronger for the Republicans. The American Party under Fillmore promised to limit the number of immigrants entering the country, but that issue lacked the excitement of the slavery question.

A Wish Fulfilled

On November 4 the American electorate expressed its choices. Buchanan received 1,838,169 votes; Fremont tallied 1,341,264, while Fillmore polled 874,534. Although Buchanan had not received a majority of popular votes cast, he captured a majority of the electoral votes. Clearly he faced an enormous challenge. He knew that his administration had "to arrest, if possible, the agitation of slavery in the North, and to destroy sectional parties." Was Buchanan the leader who could do this? Only time would tell.

Chapter 9

Struggling for Solutions

Wednesday, March 4, 1857. A bright morning sun greeted the assemblage gathered on the east portico of the Capitol to observe the inauguration of the 15th President of the United States. The light breeze that cooled the crowd hinted more of spring than a leftover from winter. The installation of a new chief executive was always a historic occasion, and this was no different.

This particular swearing-in carried its own memorable footnote: at age 65, James Buchanan was the oldest man to become President, while at age 36, John Breckinridge was the youngest to become Vice-President. But few people who sat and stood on the east portico that March morning were concerned about historic footnotes. Instead, they were keenly concerned about what the new President might say regarding his plans for the nation's future.

INSTILLING NEW FAITH

No one understood the importance of a strong beginning more than James Buchanan himself. As a veteran of over 40 years of public service, he was keenly aware of how important positive first impressions were. The troubled times of the nation cast a somber shadow over the entire country. The issue of slavery had divided family and friends. There was talk of states leaving the Union, of war. It was to such a concerned audience that James Buchanan spoke, hoping to instill new faith in the nation. His voice was firm as he stood at the inaugural podium.

"Our present financial condition is without parallel in history," Buchanan told those gathered at his inauguration. Surely, he reasoned, people would be reassured in knowing that their nation was financially secure. What person is not happier feeling a few dollars in his pocket? Hoping to excite his audience with thoughts of even a greater nation, geographically, Buchanan announced his intentions to try purchasing both Cuba and Alaska. Certainly, the mood of the moment was wrapped around the thought that "bigger is better." What American would not enjoy the prospects of more lands and territories?

Buchanan spoke of his own indebtedness to those who had given him the opportunity to lead the country he cherished, but he promised that he would serve just one term so that others might have their fair chance. This news, Buchanan thought to himself, would likely please such political rivals as Stephen Douglas and Lewis Cass, who wanted the presidency so much for themselves.

Finally, Buchanan touched nimbly on the slavery issue itself, referring to the bitter dispute in Kansas and the case involving the slave Dred Scott. Such matters did not belong in the executive or legislative arenas to settle, Buchanan observed, but in the judicial body. Such disputes were to be settled by the Supreme Court, and "to their decision, in common with all good citizens, I shall cheerfully submit, whatever this may be."

The gala parade at Buchanan's inauguration included a model of a ship to commemorate Admiral Peary's contact with Japan, opening that area to trade. (Library of Congress.)

PROBLEMS FOR THE PRESIDENT

Buchanan always relied on the Constitution of the United States as the nation's cornerstone, and on the Supreme Court to interpret the rights and freedoms therein. He had hoped that some day he might serve as a justice in that esteemed body, but that was never to be. Well, if he could not be a member of the Supreme Court, he would do everything possible as President of the United States to support its decisions. Never in his wildest dreams could James Buchanan imagine an unfair verdict emanating from that august body of jurists. Nor did he believe that the American people would ever rise in disagreement to a decision rendered by that Court.

But two days after Buchanan's inauguration, an uproar swept across the nation when the Supreme Court ruled that as a slave, Dred Scott was not an American citizen, had no rights, and that the Missouri Compromise of 1820 was null and void. Even southern congressmen who hailed the proslavery decision of the Supreme Court questioned the judges' right to nullify acts of the national legislature. "The members of our highest judicial body should stay out of politics!" Henry Clay blasted. "They are to solve our problems, not make them."

The Slavery Issue in Kansas

President Buchanan realized that he had overestimated the ability of the Supreme Court to always render fair decisions. Therefore, he decided to play more of an active role regarding the problems in Kansas. For years, the people of that territory had been fighting over whether to be admitted to the Union as a free state or as a slave state. Proslavery forces had won the state legislature (not without considerable vote fraud) and passed laws supporting the owning of slaves. One law allowed people to be sent to prison for two years for merely questioning the system, while another law sentenced people to death who were found guilty of encouraging slaves to run away.

In Lecompton, Kansas, the proslavery backers met to write up a state constitution that could be submitted to the national Congress for admission to the Union. Those favoring Kansas' entry as a free state (the "Free-Soilers") refused to attend the Lecompton meeting. Nevertheless, the Lecompton constitution was sent to Washington.

Fearful that their state might enter the Union as a slave state, the Free-Soilers organized and elected their own representatives to their state legislature. When brought up for a vote in the legislature, the Lecompton constitution was defeated.

Nonetheless, Buchanan wanted to get the matter settled as expeditiously as possible. He pushed Congress forward, wanting it to admit Kansas to the Union under the Lecompton constitution. If nothing else, the Dred Scott decision had revealed that Congress had no right to rule against the owning of slaves as property. It was in the United States Constitution, after all, and if the people of Kansas chose to amend their own state constitution at some later date, that could be done. "But we must end this bloodshed," Buchanan insisted.

Once more President Buchanan made a serious miscalculation. Naturally, the Republicans immediately opposed the Lecompton constitution, cynically labeling Buchanan as "that Pennsylvanian from the South." Among the Democrats, Stephen Douglas raised his voice as much in criticism against Buchanan and his "personal meddling" as against anything else. Douglas not only managed to divide his own political party into proslavery and antislavery sides, he also managed to leave the President with virtually no support in his own party. The Lecompton constitution squeaked by the Senate but was voted down by the House. Returned to Kansas, the document was defeated by the voters, six to one.

Financial Worries

Surprised and disappointed by the rulings of the Supreme Court and personally refuted by his own party for his efforts to resolve the slavery issue, by the autumn of 1857 Buchanan found himself caught up in another serious situation. In the immediate aftermath of the Mexican-American War, the nation's economy thrived. Industries were born, the wheat belt expanded, railroads snaked across the country in every direction. But the collapse of the Ohio Life Insurance Company triggered the end of the postwar "boom" in America. If a company so outwardly secure as Ohio Life could fail, what was to stop other financial concerns from collapsing?

The isolated Ohio Life problem quickly spread from the Ohio Valley into the eastern urban centers, bringing unemployment and breadlines. The surplus in the federal Treasury was soon reduced to nothing, and before the devastation was over, the nation was over $27 million in debt. The entire depression had a much greater effect in the North than the South, contributing to the ever-increasing social unrest and bitterness in the country.

Bickering in the Cabinet

With problems besieging him from all sides, Buchanan tried hard to work for harmony within his Cabinet. But he soon discovered that his careful balancing of three northerners, three southerners, and one border state (Tennessee) representative only made for constant bickering. Each idea, no matter who presented it, was weighed with much suspicion. "I had hoped we might work as a team," Buchanan reminded those at the table around him, but his voice was a feeble cry in a thunderstorm. There were times when meetings adjourned because of shouts and threats, hardly the atmosphere Buchanan hoped to maintain.

Thankfully, Harriet Lane offered some respite from the confusion and mounting tension. As the nation's First Lady, she gracefully hosted both private and public gatherings and never seemd to tire of making conversation with visiting dignitaries. Newspaper reporters labeled her "Our Democratic Queen," and she fared far better in the press than her uncle did. "Would that I could hand over the Presidency to my niece," Buchanan told a confidant, "I think the majority of Americans would approve."

Growing Hostilities

Sadly, the growing hostility between North and South hampered Buchanan's efforts to improve relations with other countries. His secretary of state, Lewis Cass, was a trained and polished politician, but he was no diplomat. Buchanan's past experience came in handy as far as working with other countries was concerned, but it required much time away from domestic duties.

Buchanan's success with Great Britain as the American minister to that country paved the way for treaties limiting England's efforts to expand its colonies in Central America. And thanks to Buchanan's keen sense of wording and timing, the inspection of foreign merchant ships by British warships was also curtailed.

From Across the Sea

There was cause for much rejoicing in August of 1858. Through the successful laying of a cable on the floor of the Atlantic Ocean, telegraph greetings were exchanged between President Buchanan of the United States and Queen Victoria of England. Wild crowds celebrating the extraordinary achievement in New York City managed to set City Hall on fire.

The 1850s, including the Buchanan presidential years, were part of a historical period called the Victorian Age. Americans, though generally satisfied with their own governmental structure, maintained a constant interest in the woman who wore the crown across the sea. She had assumed the throne in 1837, when she was only 18 years old, and her likes and dislikes affected styles and tastes far beyond the boundaries of her own sovereignty.

American architects reflected a Victorian flavor in their buildings, enjoying ornate but useless towers, countless windows, sweeping porches, and fancy "gingerbread" trim. Inside homes, rooms were equally cluttered with chairs, tables, statues, plants, lamps, and knickknacks. Only those with thin figures and frames could navigate a room without fear of bumping into something.

But those Americans imitating Victorian styles were far from slender. It was said that Queen Victoria herself enjoyed formal dinners that could include up to 12 courses. The

1850s were times for hearty eating and little exercise. Despite his own reputation for impeccable dress, President Buchanan was also known for enjoying elegant dinner parties with cuisine of festive proportions.

THE LINCOLN–DOUGLAS DEBATES

But such accomplishments by President Buchanan went largely unnoticed. He always appeared to be backing away from any confrontation, hiding from taking a forceful stand. In 1858, when Stephen Douglas, a Democrat, and Abraham Lincoln, a Republican, sought a Senate seat from the state of Illinois, the two men conducted a series of debates that began in August and ran into October. Their seven encounters attracted national interest.

Dubbed "The Little Giant" because of his fiery oratory, Douglas stood but five feet tall and dressed with flair and style. Lincoln, on the other hand, was a full six-foot-four, spoke with a country accent, and wore trousers that did not touch his shoes and coats with sleeves that did not reach his wrists. Yet it was the ideas proposed by Douglas and Lincoln that demanded that Americans, including Buchanan, consider their position on the slavery issue.

Lincoln clearly felt that slavery was "a moral, a social and a political wrong." However, he did not suggest it be abolished where it was already in existence. He simply opposed the spread of slavery into any new state. For Douglas, slavery was neither right nor wrong and it should be determined by popular sovereignty. "It is the people living in a new state who should decide whether or not they wish slavery to exist."

Recognizing that the people were not happy with Buchanan, Douglas used the debates to criticize the President for not exercising leadership. In the end, it was Douglas who won the senatorial post, but it was Lincoln's warning that "a house divided against itself cannot stand," and his belief that the "government cannot endure permanently half slave and half free" that caused Americans to ponder the nation's future. The recurring thought that the Union could split apart kept James Buchanan awake many nights.

CAUSE FOR CELEBRATION

The completion of a transatlantic cable between the United States and Great Britain afforded some cause for celebration. Greetings and congratulations were extended from Her Majesty Queen Victoria to Buchanan, and a warm reply was sent back. "It is a triumph more glorious, because far more useful to mankind, than was ever won by conqueror on the field of battle," observed the American leader. He then added, "May the Atlantic telegraph, under the blessing of Heaven, prove to be a bond of perpetual peace and friendship between the kindred nations, and an instrument destined by Divine Providence to diffuse religion, civilization, liberty and law throughout the world."

But the occasions for celebration were few. In ordinary times, James Buchanan might have been able to use his ability as an able compromiser to pull together the ever-dividing factions of the nation. Clearly, however, the times were anything but ordinary. Dark clouds were forming on the horizon, clouds destined to bring destruction. Try as he could, the President of the United States seemed helpless against the gathering doom.

Chapter 10

Triumphs and Tragedies

While the criticisms and complaints in Congress grew ever louder against "that jellyfish in the White House," an incident early in 1859 gave President Buchanan an opportunity to display forceful executive leadership. Newspapers, filled with daily stories of debate over the slavery issue, gave little space and attention to an event that occurred in Paraguay.

A SHOW OF FORCE

Traditionally, American ships had enjoyed full freedom of the waterways of South America. Naval ships made frequent excursions along the rivers in order to determine their navigability. Permission was never requested because it was not thought to be needed. However, Paraguay's President Lopez took exception to such a policy and notified his military staff to challenge any foreign vessel sailing inside the country's borders.

When a U.S. steamer, the *Water Witch*, made its way up the Parana River in Paraguay, it was stopped. In a moment of confusion, a Paraguayan soldier fired on the foreign vessel and killed the helmsman. American naval authorities were outraged and demanded immediate retaliation.

President Buchanan immediately decided to show a maximum amount of force. He not only wanted to flex American military might in the faces of Paraguayan leaders, but also to suitably impress the entire Western Hemisphere. Nineteen ships carrying 2,500 U.S. Marines and sailors were sent at once to the area, causing a shocked Lopez to issue an apology and sign an agreement that no such situation would ever happen again. It was one of a beleaguered President's finer moments.

ABOLITIONIST JOHN BROWN

By contrast, the actions of abolitionist John Brown captured headlines across the nation later that same year. It was not the first time people had read about Brown, for he had made news over three years before during the "bleeding Kansas" period. Missouri settlers in favor of slavery frequently crossed territorial lines into Kansas, threatening the antislavery residents.

A strong abolitionist, Brown and seven other men (including four of his own sons and a son-in-law) attacked a proslavery settlement at Pottawatomie Creek in Kansas and murdered five men, leaving their bodies as a warning to slavery supporters. In the years that followed, Brown raised funds to help runaway slaves and those fighting slavery. To many northerners, Brown was a brave hero.

The Raid at Harper's Ferry

Deciding to take his campaign into the heart of slave country, in the fall of 1859 Brown turned a farm into a fortress some four miles outside of Harper's Ferry, Virginia, the site of a federal arsenal. On the night of October 16, he led a group of 18 men, including five blacks, on a raid of the arsenal. Plans called for slaves in the area to join in the attack, but none did.

News of the raid traveled quickly. Government action was equally swift. Colonel Robert E. Lee was sent with a battalion of U.S. Marines to recapture the federal arsenal. In the skirmish that followed, four local citizens, including the mayor of Harper's Ferry and a free black, were killed. Ten of John Brown's men were also killed, including two of his sons.

Brown was caught and put on trial for treason against the state of Virginia and for inciting a slave uprising. Across the nation, people argued Brown's innocence or guilt. No comments came from the White House. As usual, James Buchanan was satisfied that the law would take proper care of the accused. Convicted of both crimes, John Brown was hanged at Charlestown, Virginia, on December 2, 1859. Finally, Buchanan issued a short statement: "Justice has been done."

Condemnation and Praise

Most Americans, including such political leaders as Stephen Douglas and Abraham Lincoln, condemned the actions of the dead abolitionist. Lincoln reaffirmed his contempt for slavery, but he would not justify "violence, bloodshed and treason" as a means of eliminating the social evil.

But Brown also had numerous defenders, some hailing him as a martyr, a champion for good. "Here was a man who accepted the rule of God over the rule of man," shouted another abolitionist, Wendell Phillips. "Since when do we accept the laws of the United States and of Virginia while ignoring the voice of the Almighty?"

While northerners debated the worthiness of John Brown's actions, southerners were shocked that his actions could be defended. "A criminal has been executed for his dastardly deeds," an editorial in one southern newspaper proclaimed, "and yet there are some who would think we have killed a saint."

When it was revealed that documents found at the arsenal included other locations in the South that John Brown planned to attack, there were many southerners who feared more of such raids. Peddlers, sailors, and teachers from northern states who were living or visiting southern states were suddenly set upon by vigilante mobs. "Are you a follower of John Brown?" they were asked. "Why are you here? What is your business?" If the answers did not come fast enough or were not correct enough to suit the interrogators, the victims were beaten. Fearing more violence from unknown sources, southerners enacted their own kind of vengeance. Brown's final words, "The crimes of this guilty land will never be purged away but with Blood," appeared to be coming true.

Deafening Silence

The silence from the White House during all this turmoil was deafening. Leaders of both political parties hoped that President Buchanan might be able to find some plan of action, or at least some comforting words, that would heal some of the wounds the nation had suffered and thus solidify the Union. But nothing came.

Aware that the Union was gradually coming apart with each passing month, Buchanan felt there was little he could do to stop it. Talk of southern states seceding (withdrawing) from the Union and forming their own government became more and more common, but the chief executive thought such a notion unbelievable.

OLD MOTHER BUCHANAN AT WHEATLAND.

As the problems between North and South intensified, threatening to pull the country apart, newspapers depicted Buchanan as a helpless old woman who could not or would not take action. (Library of Congress.)

Buchanan continued to maintain his regular daily schedule, working from eight until one, lunching, then working again until five. Guests continued to visit him in his office, but they always came on official business. There was no lighthearted banter, no personal or political friends stopping by. That was restricted to state and Cabinet dinners held weekly and hosted by niece Harriet.

At times the somber mood of the world outside reflected itself in the social gatherings at the White House despite Harriet Lane's dedicated efforts to maintain cheerful conversation. No dancing was allowed, due in part to those outside the White House who might take exception to such recreation as being too "frivolous."

Buchanan found that the $25,000 annual salary he received did not always stretch (there was no special funding for official entertaining). Therefore, it was occasionally necessary to draw upon his own private finances in order to pay the bills. Nonetheless, it was clearly understood that "the old man" in the White House would not accept any gifts from outside sources for fear that such a custom would lead to speculation of an exchange of favors.

A PRINCELY VISIT

News that England's Prince of Wales would be visiting Canada sometime during 1860 brightened President Buchanan's spirits. If he had achieved nothing else, he was proud of the fact that American relationships with Great Britain had been strengthened. His invitation to the prince to visit the United States in addition to Canada was cheerfully accepted, and Washington society readied itself to impress the royal visitor.

For a short time in October, political bickering gave way to a nonstop schedule of entertaining with the prince in constant demand as a guest of honor. One of the most elaborate affairs was planned and hosted by Harriet Lane as she took the royal party on a steamer trip to see Mount Vernon. Champagne flowed, exotic foods filled giant tables, and once more there was laughter in the air.

Even the newspapers found space to praise the President for knowing "exactly how to entertain foreign dignitaries." One Washington editor, unable to restrain a wistful note, observed that "it would be grand indeed if our elected leader knew as much about executing the internal affairs of the nation as he apparently knows about hosting leaders from abroad."

The visit of the Prince of Wales was virtually the only bright spot during the final year of Buchanan's presidency, and it lasted but a fleeting moment. He was a political mystery, lambasted (criticized) by his own political party as well as by adversarial foes for a multitude of incompetencies. Northerners thought him too much a southerner; southerners thought him too northern. He was caught in a vise-like squeeze.

It was difficult enough having to endure the comments and criticisms that found their way into speeches delivered in Congress or into newspaper articles. But to make matters worse, in the spring of 1860 President Buchanan was the subject of a congressional investigation that left him totally devastated. "No man should have to endure such torture," Buchanan wrote, and by the end of the year he longed to be free of the office that he had sought so eagerly.

Chapter 11
A Nation Divides

The mood of Washington in the early months of 1860 was ugly indeed. Southern congressmen in both the House of Representatives and the Senate felt put upon, victims of scorn and abuse. People who had never been to their part of the country, never enjoyed the warmth and hospitality of which they were so proud, based their opinions of the southern way of life on what they had read in Harriet Beecher Stowe's novel, *Uncle Tom's Cabin*.

Southerners complained that the book seemed to turn slaves into saints and their owners into devils. Why couldn't northerners understand that slavery was an economic necessity, that slaveowners did not roam plantations looking for a black to whip? If matters did not change, if the situation did not improve, many southern leaders were convinced that the South would be better off on its own.

There were many northerners who sympathized with the southern position; if certain southern states wished to leave the Union, let it be done peacefully. But the majority of northerners viewed slavery as a basic evil, socially, morally, politically, or in whatever spectrum. Whether that opinion was formed through reading a book, hearing a plaintive tale of a runaway slave, or engaging in philosophical arguments, more people became convinced that one man owning another was definitely wrong and should be changed. At all costs, the Union should be preserved.

The "Little Lady" with the Mighty Pen

Harriet Beecher Stowe hardly looked like a troublemaker. Clusters of curls framed a round face, set off by deep-set eyes, a prominent nose, and thin lips. Always appropriately attired for the wife of a professor of Biblical literature, her modest dresses could not hide the more than ample figure. When she spoke, her voice was soft but firm, always in control and curt with conviction.

No, it was not the outward appearance of Harriet Beecher Stowe that made any noticeable impact; in a gathering, she might easily be overlooked. It was in her writing that this woman made her presence felt. From the moment Stowe's *Uncle Tom's Cabin* appeared in print, it aroused the mind and spirit of Americans everywhere, fanning abolitionist sparks into flames.

Upon meeting Mrs. Stowe at the White House during the Civil War, President Abraham Lincoln observed, "So this is the little lady who made this big war." Of course, the Civil War cannot be attributed to any one person or one event. But few books in literature have done more to stir up public opinion and cause political squabbling.

The daughter of a minister and sister to five more, Harriet was surrounded by those who rejected slavery in every sense. "We are all children of God," she declared often, "and He alone is our Master." Her early years were spent in Cincinnati, Ohio, and excursions across the river into Kentucky left her

Scenes like this one showing the separation of mother and child from Harriet Beecher Stowe's book, Uncle Tom's Cabin, *heightened antislavery feelings across the nation.* (Library of Congress.)

repulsed at the relationships she witnessed between slaves and their owners.

Moving to Maine in 1850, Harriet learned of the trauma experienced by runaway slaves, always looking over their shoulder for those on their trail. Her husband and the rest of her family encouraged her to share her feelings on paper. After *Uncle Tom's Cabin* first appeared as a magazine serial in 1852, it was quickly rushed into book form. Millions gobbled up copies, weeping over the sympathetic

Uncle Tom and little Eva, while despising the horrible slaveowner Simon Legree. A children's adaptation was printed, and a stage play performed. More than a million copies were sold in the British Empire, and many British readers commented wryly about the so-called American freedom that "those bloody colonists" had fought a war to achieve.

While *Uncle Tom's Cabin* increased anti-slavery sentiment above the Mason-Dixon Line, Stowe's literary creation was openly denounced in the South. "Harriet Beecher Stowe casts shame on every aspect of our day-to-day living," noted one newspaper editor in Atlanta. "She would have the world view slavery as a criminal disease rather than a mere economic necessity."

Perhaps the importance of *Uncle Tom's Cabin* rests in the fact that for the first time the issue of slavery was put into human, personal terms. Whether or not the institution of slavery should exist had been debated before, but as readers became caught up in the lives of Stowe's characters, fictional as they were, people were driven to argument and action. "This can't continue," many northerners insisted. "Vicious lies and distortions!" countered the southerners. "Leave us alone!"

Uncle Tom's Cabin was but one complicated piece in the jigsaw puzzle of history that became the Civil War. As for Harriet Beecher Stowe, she continued to write with a crusading zeal. A book about Great Britain's

revered poet, Lord Byron, and his question-
able relationship with his sister caused a furor
across the sea. ''I hardly think Mrs. Stowe
would have been privy [given access to] to
such knowledge,'' an austere Queen Victoria
noted. England's leading novelist, Charles
Dickens, was outraged. ''I would like to see
Mrs. Stowe in a pillory [stocks used for
punishment],'' he declared.

Despite such criticisms, Harriet Beecher
Stowe enjoyed a long, successful career as a
writer. She died in 1896 at the age of 85.

SEEKING A SCAPEGOAT

Within this atmosphere of discontent arose one overriding
thought — someone had to accept responsibility. It was not
enough to merely blame the current situation on the institution of slavery itself. No, a human scapegoat for the nation's
woes was needed. What better choice than "the old man" in
the White House, who appeared to have offended everyone
by his inability to provide leadership to resolve the emotional
conflict that was dividing the land?

James Buchanan seemed to be a confused collection of
contradictions. One moment he would talk of his personal
contempt for slavery; the next, he would argue that
southerners should be left alone because the Constitution protected their right to own slaves. "We must preserve the Union,"
the chief executive would proclaim, yet he seemed oblivious
to the fact that the Union was rapidly crumbling.

In the Lecompton affair, Buchanan had clearly supported
a state constitution opposed by the people. He had also

challenged the ideas of his own party leader, Stephen Douglas. And he had encouraged the nation to follow the concepts of its own Constitution, yet he himself failed to display the sterling leadership qualities of the men who had written the document. Surely, enough was enough.

A CONGRESSIONAL INVESTIGATION

On March 5, 1860, a resolution was introduced on the House floor by John Covode, a congressman from Pennsylvania, calling for an official investigation of President Buchanan, his affairs, and his administration. The investigation would be "secret," but it was certainly implied that if evidence of misconduct should turn up, impeachment proceedings (legal charges) would follow. The resolution passed quickly, and five House members were appointed to conduct the investigation. For the first time in American history, a committee was set up to look for misdeeds by a U.S. President.

Buchanan was incensed. Certainly he knew that many of his efforts as chief executive had not succeeded, but the suggestion of misconduct on his part was insulting and humiliating. From his own perspective, no one had struggled harder to keep the Union together, to maintain law and order, to promote restraint and compromise in the face of frenzied oratory and wild reaction. How dare the House of Representatives demand such an investigation, with the accuser, John Covode, from his own native state no less, serving as chairman of the committee to evaluate the actions of the President? The entire investigation, Buchanan wrote in a letter to the House, "is as vague and general as the English language affords words in which to make it."

But the House members paid little attention to Buchanan's objections. Some wanted political blood, and the trail led to the White House. After all, this was an election year, and the Republicans believed anything that would taint Buchanan would also taint the entire Democratic Party.

Senator Stephen Douglas watched the House investigation carefully. He had safely distanced himself from any association with the chief executive and was already developing a program to lead "a new, fair and caring, Democratic Party" into the White House. For the most part, Buchanan stood alone, with only a handful of staunch party faithfuls willing to share his burden.

Looking for Evidence

All during the spring the Covode investigation committee interviewed government employees and political colleagues of the chief executive. Reports and papers were examined carefully, each word and phrase being analyzed for double meaning or devious intent. The committee tried to determine if Buchanan had used his office to dispense patronage jobs to undeserving individuals, or perhaps improper influence had been applied to persuade congressmen to vote a certain way on a certain bill. Were the financial records in order? Could Buchanan be charged with failure to execute the laws of the land? Had he misused government property?

The longer the investigation continued, the angrier Buchanan became. "There is nothing impartial and just about these proceedings," he declared. "This is a political inquisition, designed to embarrass me and my administration, and it is disgraceful that the House of Representatives would allow such a disgusting thing to happen!"

In the middle of the Covode investigation, a few loyal supporters and one reporter asked Buchanan if he might reconsider his earlier pledge not to run for re-election. "We know you had said you would not be a candidate again," the newspaperman queried, "but politicians, once in office, have been known to change their minds. Have you given any thought to reconsidering?" Buchanan smiled. "I shall have a statement for you tomorrow."

When the reporter returned the next day, Buchanan handed him the promise he made when he gave his inaugural address: "Having determined not to become a candidate for reelection, I shall have no motive to influence my conduct in administering the government except the desire ably and faithfully to serve my country, and to live in the grateful memory of my countrymen."

No Evidence of Misbehavior

By the middle of June, the Covode committee had completed its investigation. Despite an intense search, they had found nothing in the way of real evidence to support any claims of misbehavior. Although the investigation was finished, Buchanan was still enraged over the entire situation. He sent a message of disgust to House members, blasting their "false and atrocious" charges, charges which ignored the good of the country while playing a game of smear politics. His communication was taken under advisement.

THE ELECTION OF 1860

A week later, the Democrats met in Baltimore and selected Stephen Douglas to champion their party cause in the November election for President. (The Republicans had already selected their candidate in May—Abraham Lincoln from the state of Illinois.) Buchanan would have nothing to do with such a choice. Instead, he threw his personal support to John

Breckinridge, the choice of the southern Democrats, who met a week later.

Once more, Buchanan publicly declared that he felt the property rights of southerners were to be protected, as the Supreme Court had decided in the Dred Scott case. To Buchanan, the question was totally a legal one, not affected by individual notions of morality.

Buchanan played no active part in the election of 1860. But he remained convinced that the flames of antislavery were fanned by a handful of northern abolitionists and that their efforts would gradually fade away. In August of 1860, he said:

> There is but one possible contingency which can endanger the Union, and against this all Democrats, whether squatter sovereigns or popular sovereigns, will present a united resistance. Should the time ever arrive when northern agitation and fanaticism shall proceed so far as to render the domestic firesides of the South insecure, then, and not till then, will the Union be in danger. A United Northern Democracy will prevent a wall of fire against such a catastrophe.

Was it wishful thinking? No, Buchanan remained certain that slavery would eventually disappear but it would do so on its own power, being abolished by those who controlled its existence. Unless the slaveowners themselves consented to abolish the practice, there was nothing the federal government could do.

SECESSION BEGINS

On election eve, Buchanan received an urgent communication from General Winfield Scott, the Army chief of staff. Scott suggested that the nine federal forts in the South be strengthened in the event Abraham Lincoln was elected. Lincoln's antislavery views were well known, and Scott feared that southerners might try to capture the forts if Lincoln won. However, feeling that such military action might provoke the South, Buchanan ignored the suggestion.

Scott's anticipation of Lincoln's victory proved true. Celebrations were held in cities across the North, while the South retreated into an eerie state of mourning. The legislature of South Carolina immediately set December 17 as a date for a state convention to discuss withdrawing from the Union. It seemed appropriate that South Carolina should lead the way because their own John C. Calhoun had fathered the "Doctrine of Nullification." This was a statement that any state had the right to withdraw from the Union when the United States followed a wrong path.

It took the elected delegates at the South Carolina convention only three days to repeal the Ordinance of 1788, by which the state had ratified the Constitution of the United States. "We joined the Union voluntarily," observed one delegate, "and now that the Union threatens the rights of the people, we voluntarily secede."

Many in the nation had feared such an action, but the actuality of it still carried shock waves. It was an agonizing blow to Buchanan, who reacted by asking Attorney General Jeremiah Black what powers the President had in case of open hostilities between state and federal authorities. Black told him that the powers rested with Congress, not the President, to deal with any individual state.

A FINAL MESSAGE

In his final message to Congress in December of 1860, Buchanan once again blamed northern troublemakers with the agitation that prevailed in the nation. It was time that states left each other alone, and for individual states to handle the issue of slavery, unhampered by outside influences. But he also scolded South Carolina and issued a warning to southern states that might be thinking about leaving the Union. His feeling was that the Union "was intended to be perpetual, and not to be annulled at the pleasure of any one of the contracting parties."

Few found Buchanan's message of any value. By January, the states of Mississippi, Florida, Alabama, Georgia, Louisiana, and Texas had followed South Carolina's march along the road to secession.

Trouble at Fort Sumter

South Carolina moved to take over federal property in their state. After all, they were no longer a part of the Union, and they considered everything in the state to be theirs. American soldiers huddled behind the walls of Fort Sumter in Charleston harbor, and when a federal steamer attempted to bring them supplies, South Carolina troops fired on the ship. Quickly, the steamer retreated.

Buchanan had already been told that the President had no power in such cases. Rather, it was up to Congress to take whatever action it deemed necessary. Most American soldiers on active duty were located out West, where they were busy defending new settlers against Indians, and no funds existed for additional troops. Furthermore, Congress had little interest in cooperating with a lame-duck President (one who is leaving office) whom most held in contempt.

On March 9, 1861, an old and weary James Buchanan picked up Abraham Lincoln in a carriage to take him to the inaugural proceedings. "If you are as happy, my dear sir, on entering this house as I am on leaving it and returning home, you are the happiest man on earth," said Buchanan.

Chapter 12

Back to Wheatland

The bands played, the bells tolled, the people cheered as James Buchanan's train rolled into the Lancaster railroad station. He was back home, among the family and friends he had known for so long. It was a good feeling.

Once again, Buchanan enjoyed the comfort and beauty of his beloved Wheatland. Gone were the papers to sign, the appointments, and the never-ending flow of official duties. Now there was time to relax with a good book and a goblet of Madeira wine. Now and then he indulged himself with a cigar and an afternoon nap. He welcomed his nephews and nieces with their children, watching as the younger tots played tag and hide-and-seek outside.

CRITICISMS AND ACCUSATIONS

But in just a few weeks the happy times came to an end. News of fighting between state and federal troops in Charleston harbor on April 12, 1861, troubled him greatly. America was at war, a civil war within itself. Adding to that tragedy was the news that many people in the North and South held Buchanan responsible. Republicans labeled him "inept, fumbling, unable to anticipate the future of his own inaction." Democrats joined in the chorus of criticism.

Not only was Buchanan attacked as a President, he was maligned as a person. Stories circulated about selling White House furniture, taking gifts from foreign visitors that were intended to be left in Washington, and misusing public funds and power. All the accusations of the Covode investigation suddenly resurfaced. Questions were even raised about Harriet Lane, once the delight of the press reporters. Had she been used in devious ways? What was her real relationship with her uncle?

In Seclusion

The rumors hurt Buchanan deeply. He was in no position to fight back. He prayed for the war to end quickly so that people might lift their spirits and look to the future. But each day brought word of increased fighting, of new deaths and injuries. Threatening notes were slipped under his door, trash strewn on his property.

No longer did the people come daily to visit the "Squire of Lancaster." And no longer did Buchanan take his carriage into the city. He was refused membership in the Presbyterian Church, and some merchants requested that his housekeeper, Miss Hetty, make her purchases elsewhere. Buchanan secluded himself at Wheatland, not wanting to face the incriminating glances of his neighbors or see their sad expressions.

But the former President could not keep out the painful letters he received. They came from North and South alike, woeful stories of sons and brothers lost on the battlefields. "Why didn't you do something to stop it?" one mother asked. "Two of my sons lie dead and their blood is on your hands." The letters were heartbreaking, and Buchanan took to his bed with a serious case of fever. When he had the strength, he scribbled notes for a book he was writing entitled *Mr. Bu-*

chanan's Administration on the Eve of Rebellion. He wanted people to hear his side, to share honestly the events that had transpired.

Lincoln Assassinated

In the election of 1864, the Democrats picked General George McClellan to take on the incumbent, Republican Abraham Lincoln. But northerners, though disappointed that the Civil War continued, were not ready to abandon the leader of the fight. The Confederate states had selected their own chief executive, Jefferson Davis, and they had little interest in the affairs of the Union. Lincoln won a resounding victory, which did not surprise Buchanan.

The assassination of the President a year later was a crushing blow to his predecessor. "I deeply mourn his loss," Buchanan said, "from private feelings, but still more deeply for the sake of the country. Heaven, I trust, will not suffer the perpetrators of the deed and all their guilty accomplices to escape just punishment."

OUT OF SECLUSION

In 1866 Buchanan completed his book and saw it published. It received little public notice, but that did not bother its author. As far as he was concerned, the record was there for anyone who wished to review what had truly occurred. It contained scant material as to his own personal defense, but to those who knew Buchanan well, that was no surprise. Satisfied that he had served his country to the best of his ability, there seemed no reason to offer contrived excuses.

Slowly, Lancaster again opened its arms to their most famous citizen. Not one to hold grudges, Buchanan returned to a routine of visiting in the city, calling on friends and family members. He took an interest in Franklin and Marshall College, as well as in local charities. Occasionally, he was sought out for his political opinions. He advised Democrats to support states' rights and oppose women's suffrage (the right to vote), basically because it was the right of the states, not the federal government, to regulate voting.

"I HAVE NO REGRET . . ."

In the fall of 1867 Buchanan fell on the porch steps at Wheatland. He never fully recovered from the accident. Shortly before his death on June 1, 1868, he told a friend, "I have always felt and still feel that I discharged every public duty imposed on me constitutionally. I have no regret for any public act of my life, and history will vindicate my memory."

News of the former President's death brought a variety of reactions as it traveled across the country. Bitter feelings remained among those who felt Buchanan might have prevented the war that had left empty chairs in many homes, bloodstains on American soil, and an ugly blemish on the pages of history. Others were more forgiving, like one newspaper editor who noted, "He was a man wedded to the Constitution of the United States and could hear no other voices than those men in Philadelphia so long ago."

Buchanan had requested a small, quiet burial. But the people of Lancaster would not hear of such a thing. James Buchanan was one of them; to some, he was their "Jimmie" and he deserved a ceremony like the ceremonious life he had lived.

In truth, there were those around Lancaster who felt remorse for the way Buchanan had been treated during and after his presidency. And because there were consciences that

Family and friends of James Buchanan gathered on June 4, 1868, to pay their final respects for the man they knew not only as President of the United States but also as "The Squire of Lancaster." (Library of Congress.)

needed cleansing, 20,000 people came to pay their final respects to the man who had served as the 15th President of the United States. He was laid to rest in a small cemetery in Lancaster.

THE BUCHANAN LEGACY

James Buchanan came to the presidency with impeccable credentials and experience. A trained lawyer, he had served in the Pennsylvania legislature, the U.S. House of Representatives and Senate, as an American minister to two major foreign powers, and as secretary of state. These were impressive achievements, to be sure.

Despite the problems confronting the nation, particularly the slavery issue, Buchanan was confident that he could provide the leadership the country needed. The presidency, after all, was not something that was suddenly thrust upon him. Quite the opposite. He had longed for the position for many years, eager to take on the duties and responsibilities of the country's highest elected office.

Always given to careful analysis of any situation, Buchanan had studied the strengths and weaknesses of those who had preceded him into the White House, especially examining their mistakes. "History is not only a course to be learned as a student," he once remarked, "but rather a teacher in itself. He who would not learn from the past is a fool destined for failure."

A Man of Remarkable Qualifications

Clearly, the Buchanan legacy is one that illustrates the immense depth and breadth of leadership required if an individual is to truly succeed as a President of the United States.

On paper, James Buchanan would appear to possess remarkable qualifications for the job of chief executive of the nation. Perhaps the finest constitutional lawyer of his time, a first-class diplomat, a true and devoted patriot, a consummate politician, a gentleman of the highest order—yet there are few who would rate him above "mediocre" as a President, and many who would rate him far lower. Shortly before his death, sensing the critical evaluation that the passage of time might give him, Buchanan expressed no regrets concerning his public life and stated that "history will vindicate my memory."

Sadly, however, that has not happened, despite some successes during Buchanan's years as President, especially in dealing with Great Britain. But the fact remains that a nation which had already started to pull apart when he took office had split completely by the time he left.

The Constitution, in Buchanan's mind, clearly protected the property of all citizens. But because he viewed slaves as property, as did the Supreme Court, he believed there was nothing the federal government could do. That he hated slavery himself was beside the point. It was not within his nature to make moral judgments for other men. Slavery was a problem of the South, and neither the North nor the President had any right to interfere.

As to maintaining the Union, Buchanan personally felt that no state had the right to secede. Yet his efforts of concession and compromise to keep the Union together failed completely. It is ironic that Buchanan's successor, Abraham Lincoln, ranks as one of the greatest Presidents in American history, and yet he rejected any compromise with the South and overrode the Constitution, although such actions led directly to the Civil War.

Perhaps historian and former President Harry S. Truman may suggest one reason for Buchanan's disappointing image in history. As Truman once said:

> When one reads the Constitution and sees only words and laws, he is missing something. The men who wrote that document used much more than their minds. They wrote it using their hearts and souls. If we read it without the same heart and soul they put into its writing, we will have only a small part of what these noble men gave us.

Perhaps, if one would accept the thinking of Truman, who himself has been ranked highly by historians evaluating the Presidents of the nation, Buchanan left behind a lesson rather than a legacy for other Presidents. It is with the understanding of that lesson and subsequently acting with it in mind that James Buchanan might well receive the vindication he so deeply desired.

Bibliography

Bailey, Thomas A. *The Pugnacious Presidents.* New York: The Free Press, 1980. A clear look at how James Buchanan's policies of concession, compromise, and Constitutionalism failed to avert the oncoming Civil War.

Barclay, Barbara. *Lamps to Light the Way.* New York: Bowmar, 1970. Swiftly and dramatically, the author highlights the 40-year ascent to the presidency by James Buchanan. Unique drawings add a special touch to this brief look at the nation's 15th chief executive.

Hoyt, Edwin P. *James Buchanan.* Chicago: Reilly & Lee, 1966. Few biographers for young or adult readers can match Hoyt's talent for objectivity and clarity. From birth to death, Buchanan's life is traced with ultimate care for factual detail.

Whitney, David C. *The American Presidents.* Garden City, New York: Doubleday, 1978. Step by step, the author traces the rise of James Buchanan to the White House. The text is clear, the style direct.

Williams, T. Harry, ed. *The Union Surrendered.* Alexandria, Virginia: Time-Life Books, 1963. One of the books in the Time-Life History of the United States series, this volume covers the period from 1849 to 1865. Buchanan's place in the events surrounding him is carefully detailed.

Index

Federalists, 19–21, 25–26, 31, 38
Fillmore, Millard, 71–72, 79, 81
Fort Snelling, 7
Fort Sumter, 109
Franklin and Marshall College, 113
"Free Soilers," 86
Fremont, John, 79, 81
Fugitive Slave Law, 70

Harper's Ferry, Virginia, 93–94
Harrisburg, Pennsylvania, 22, 32
Harrison, William Henry, 53, 56
Hopkins, James, 18–19

Jackson, Andrew, 40, 42–43, 46,
    49, 51
Jefferson, Thomas, 19
Johnson, Samuel, 13
Judiciary Act of 1789, 45
Judiciary Square, 3

King, John, 16
"Know Nothings" (American Party),
    79

Lancaster County Dragoons, 20–21
Lancaster County, Pennsylvania, 21
Lancaster Journal (newspaper), 43
Lancaster, Pennsylvania, 6, 18–19,
    25, 28, 30, 32, 46, 48, 58–59,
    67, 69, 112
Landrick, Edward, 48
Lane, Harriet, 4–5, 10, 75, 88,
    96–97, 110
Lecompton, Kansas, 86
Lee, Robert E., 94
Lincoln, Abraham, 35, 90–91, 94,
    106–110, 116
Lord Byron, 103

Madison, James, 12, 27
Magaw, James, 14
Manifest Destiny, 63

Marcy, William, 74
McClellan, George, 112
McLane, Louis, 64
Mercersburg Academy, 11, 36
Mercersburg, Pennsylvania, 10, 21, 30
Mexican-American War, 61–66, 87
Milton, John, 13
Missouri Compromise, 8–9, 36, 71, 85
Monroe, James, 33, 39
*Mr. Buchanan's Administration on
    the Eve of Rebellion* (book),
    111–112

National Bank of the United States, 27

Ohio Life Insurance Company, 87
Old Stone Academy, 15
Ordinance of 1788, 108
Oregon Territory, 61–64
Ostend Manifesto, 78

Pakenham, Richard, 63–64
Panic of 1837, 54, 57
Phillips, Wendall, 94
Pierce, Benjamin, 2
Pierce, Franklin, 2, 5, 72–73, 78
Pierce, Jane, 2
Polk, James Knox, 58–65, 77
Pope, Alexander, 13
Prince Albert, 75
Prince of Wales, 97–98

Queen Victoria, 75–77, 89, 91

Randolph, John, 47
Revolutionary War, 26
Ridgeley, Charles, 20
Rush, Richard, 44

Sanford, John, 8
Scott, Dred, 7–9, 83, 85–86
Scott, Winfield, 2, 63–65, 72, 107–108
Sharon, James, 14

PRESIDENTS OF THE UNITED STATES

GEORGE WASHINGTON	L. Falkof	0-944483-19-4
JOHN ADAMS	R. Stefoff	0-944483-10-0
THOMAS JEFFERSON	R. Stefoff	0-944483-07-0
JAMES MADISON	B. Polikoff	0-944483-22-4
JAMES MONROE	R. Stefoff	0-944483-11-9
JOHN QUINCY ADAMS	M. Greenblatt	0-944483-21-6
ANDREW JACKSON	R. Stefoff	0-944483-08-9
MARTIN VAN BUREN	R. Ellis	0-944483-12-7
WILLIAM HENRY HARRISON	R. Stefoff	0-944483-54-2
JOHN TYLER	L. Falkof	0-944483-60-7
JAMES K. POLK	M. Greenblatt	0-944483-04-6
ZACHARY TAYLOR	D. Collins	0-944483-17-8
MILLARD FILLMORE	K. Law	0-944483-61-5
FRANKLIN PIERCE	F. Brown	0-944483-25-9
JAMES BUCHANAN	D. Collins	0-944483-62-3
ABRAHAM LINCOLN	R. Stefoff	0-944483-14-3
ANDREW JOHNSON	R. Stevens	0-944483-16-X
ULYSSES S. GRANT	L. Falkof	0-944483-02-X
RUTHERFORD B. HAYES	N. Robbins	0-944483-23-2
JAMES A. GARFIELD	F. Brown	0-944483-63-1
CHESTER A. ARTHUR	R. Stevens	0-944483-05-4
GROVER CLEVELAND	D. Collins	0-944483-01-1
BENJAMIN HARRISON	R. Stevens	0-944483-15-1
WILLIAM McKINLEY	D. Collins	0-944483-55-0
THEODORE ROOSEVELT	R. Stefoff	0-944483-09-7
WILLIAM H. TAFT	L. Falkof	0-944483-56-9
WOODROW WILSON	D. Collins	0-944483-18-6
WARREN G. HARDING	A. Canadeo	0-944483-64-X
CALVIN COOLIDGE	R. Stevens	0-944483-57-7

HERBERT C. HOOVER	B. Polikoff	0-944483-58-5
FRANKLIN D. ROOSEVELT	M. Greenblatt	0-944483-06-2
HARRY S. TRUMAN	D. Collins	0-944483-00-3
DWIGHT D. EISENHOWER	R. Ellis	0-944483-13-5
JOHN F. KENNEDY	L. Falkof	0-944483-03-8
LYNDON B. JOHNSON	L. Falkof	0-944483-20-8
RICHARD M. NIXON	R. Stefoff	0-944483-59-3
GERALD R. FORD	D. Collins	0-944483-65-8
JAMES E. CARTER	D. Richman	0-944483-24-0
RONALD W. REAGAN	N. Robbins	0-944483-66-6
GEORGE H.W. BUSH	R. Stefoff	0-944483-67-4

GARRETT EDUCATIONAL CORPORATION
130 EAST 13TH STREET
ADA, OK 74820